# Embracing Our Fragmented Selves

## A Workbook for Trauma Survivors and Therapists

Janina Fisher, PhD

EMBRACING OUR FRAGMENTED SELVES



Published by
PESI Publishing, Inc.
3839 White Ave
Eau Claire, WI 54703

Cover and interior design by Emily Dyer
Editing by Jenessa Jackson, PhD, and Miriam Ramos

ISBN 9781683738916 (print)
ISBN 9781683738923 (ePUB)
ISBN 9781683738930 (ePDF)



Printed in the United States of America.

PESI Publishing
pesipublishing.com

# *Praise for* Embracing Our Fragmented Selves

"There are few who have the breadth and depth of clinical expertise as Janina Fisher. Her warmth, intelligence, and open-hearted desire to help society's most traumatized individuals has been a true gift to our field and to the world. In her new book, *Embracing Our Fragmented Selves*, Janina brings together decades of clinical experience in a clear, practical, easy-to-access way that will surely benefit clinicians and trauma survivors alike."

**—Frank Anderson, MD,** author of *Transcending Trauma* and *To Be Loved*

"Dr. Janina Fisher's *Embracing Our Fragmented Selves* will be a beacon for therapists who work with trauma survivors. It's a wise and compassionate guide, filled with practical strategies, worksheets, and decades of clinical experience. This isn't just a workbook—it's a true gift for therapists and anyone seeking to reclaim a sense of wholeness."

**—David Kessler,** author of *Finding Meaning* and *Finding Meaning Workbook* and founder of Grief.com

"When it comes to treating complex PTSD and dissociation, the work of Dr. Janina Fisher has always been my most reliable and trustworthy source of wisdom and guidance. Her perspective on fragmentation not only provides compassion for survivors but also an optimistic road map for healing. In her latest book, the blending of somatic and parts work therapies provides the basis for a felt sense of wholeness, which is the birthright of us all, no matter how wounded we have been."

**—Arielle Schwartz, PhD,** psychologist, award-winning author of *The Post-Traumatic Growth Guidebook*, and founder of the Center for Resilience Informed Therapy®

"This wise, compassionate, strengths-based, and trauma-informed book is an absolute gem and a necessity for clinicians and their clients. The parts perspective, integrative approaches, and clients' stories woven into Janina's beautifully organized work illustrate creative coping strategies, including structural dissociation, fragmentation, and self-destructive behaviors that are necessary for survival. Therapists will learn how to guide clients in achieving reparative attachment experiences by acknowledging, befriending, bringing empathy to, and collaborating with their parts. The worksheet pages and journal prompts provide invaluable, non-shaming psychoeducation to help clients gain clarity, access self-compassion, celebrate resilience, and deepen genuine healing."

**—Lisa Ferentz, LCSW-C, DAPA,** author of *Letting Go of Self-Destructive Behaviors: A Workbook of Hope and Healing*

"Grounded in sound theory and rich with a career's worth of clinical insight, this workbook is a must-have companion for both survivors and therapists seeking to understand and engage protector parts and extend internal relational repair to younger, wounded selves. Whether you are standing at the threshold of healing or guiding someone through it, this book invites you to meet your inner world with patience, curiosity, and care."

**—Daphne Fatter, PhD,** author of *Integrating IFS (Internal Family Systems) into EMDR Therapy: The Step-by-Step Guide to Complex Trauma Recovery*

This book was inspired by the survivors of
trauma with whom I've had the privilege of
working for over 44 years of clinical practice.
Thank you all for being my teachers.

# Table of Contents

## SECTION II ▪ DEVELOPING RELATIONSHIP: Building Awareness, Trust, and Communication with Our Parts



## SECTION III ▪ DEEPENING: Increasing Compassion by Understanding Attachment Trauma's Complex Impact

# Acknowledgments

Every book is the product of a village, and this one is no exception.

Who founded the village? My friend and colleague Bessel van der Kolk blazed a pathway for traumatized people throughout the world beginning at a time before the mental health world recognized traumatic events. In those days, the word trauma was applied only to combat veterans and sexual assault survivors. Thanks to his tireless determination to research and develop new treatments for trauma, we now recognize that physical abuse, not just sexual abuse, has traumatic effects. Our field has grown, and our ways of helping are better than they were 20 to 30 years ago, in part because Bessel would never accept that we knew enough or had found all the best treatments. He still doesn't.

At heart of the village, I owe a huge debt of gratitude to Miriam Ramos, who collaborated on each and every page. Her voice runs throughout every page of the book. Miriam is the kind of editor you can only dream to have by your side. As a therapist, she knows trauma work, and she knows how to help authors write better than they ever thought they could. A deep bow to Miriam and undying thankfulness for her support.

I also want to thank Audrey Fortin for helping me to develop so many of the ideas and concepts that inform this book. Her insight and wisdom over the years have helped me to help hundreds of survivors, and her collaboration is reflected on every page.

The respected elders in the village are the TIST senior facilitators who mentor and certify TIST graduates. I've known these wonderful close colleagues for 5 to 30 years, and I trust them absolutely. A deep bow to Terry Trotter, Carla Hancock, Sally Lograsso, Phyllis Lorenz, Tiff Kopp, Clayre Sessoms, Karen Chadwick, Rui Cang, Jon Lee, Vita Golub-Ginsberg, Donna Swedosh, Raina Wickham, and Robyn Warbuton. I am so glad to have them by my side!

My wonderful family of friends deserves credit too. To Lana Epstein, Stephanie Ross, Deb Spragg, Frank Anderson, Lisa Ferentz, and Benjamin Fry: You lift me up, help me physically and mentally, make me laugh, and inspire me to be smarter and kinder. Without your encouragement, I would not have written a single book, much less four.

And then let me not forget the most important people of all! My sons, Jason and Jadu Jagel, my amazing daughters-in-law, Kelli Yon and Wendy Cross, and my beautiful granddaughters, Ruby, Nika, and Kaira, are the light of my life. Their love and support means the world to me.

# Introduction to Trauma-Informed Stabilization Treatment (TIST)

Since I began to specialize in trauma more than 35 years ago, I've been on a mission to find treatment strategies that worked for survivors. So often, the approaches we offered were overwhelming or threatening to them. Some survivors lacked the capacity to tolerate their emotions; some could not recall what happened without going into flashbacks. What was clear to me is that, as a therapist, it was my job to treat the individual, not to be successful using the treatment model. We needed treatment models not just for those who could tolerate them but for those who couldn't.

In 2012, I was offered an unparalleled opportunity. Senior staff at a state hospital and mental health system in the state of Connecticut asked me to develop a trauma treatment model for them that would address the issues posed by a group of highly self-destructive patients who had been institutionalized for many years. Some of them had been violent toward staff members, but the majority attacked their own bodies. Some were at such an elevated risk that they had to be accompanied by a staff member 24 hours a day to prevent self-injury. Expensive and frustrating to care for, these patients were frequently disliked. They were labeled *attention-seeking* and *manipulative*; their emotional pain was dismissed. The only treatment offered was for their behavior, not for their distress or trauma.

Both hospital and patients needed a treatment model that made sense of their behavior and their difficulty in making progress. From a trauma perspective, it was easy to see what was happening. These individuals were confined in a tightly controlled institutional setting and dependent on professionals who judged their behavior but did not understand them. This situation was extremely retraumatizing. Their attacks on their own bodies (or on staff members) could be understood as triggered responses.

These individuals could not regulate their instinctively mobilized survival defenses—fight or flight—when their bodies felt unsafe. Their ability to think clearly about the consequences of their actions was unavailable to them because traumatic activation inhibits the prefrontal cortex, or Thinking Brain. Sometimes, they begged to be discharged and to live a normal life, and other times, they tried to run away. Staff were puzzled and felt manipulated. They regretted believing that their patients wanted help when they acted out over and over again, as if they had no commitment to safety.

What the staff could not see was that these patients were fragmented and caught in an internal battle between parts of them that wanted to live and thrive versus parts that wanted to fight to the death or flee. They were poster children for a trauma model called the Structural Dissociation Model.

This theory (described in more detail in chapter 2) is grounded in neuroscience findings that our brains are organized to split or fragment under stress. The protocol we developed for the hospital was simple and structured, based on this theory, but it was compassion-focused rather than behaviorally focused. In the Structural Dissociation Model, the parts are understood to be driven by survival defense responses instinctively stimulated in situations that feel threatening.

I developed the treatment model requested by the state of Connecticut piece by piece as a small group of staff members worked with me to build on this idea. This integrative approach combined the Structural Dissociation Model as a theoretical foundation with mindfulness-based techniques focused on reinterpreting the patients' distressing emotions and self-destructive impulses as trauma-related parts. Interventions drawn from Internal Family Systems (Schwartz & Sweezy, 2020) and Ego State Therapy (Phillips & Fredericks, 1995) contributed to the work with these parts, and ideas from Sensorimotor Psychotherapy (Ogden, 2021; Ogden & Fisher, 2015) provided somatic techniques to regulate trauma responses.

The first step we took was to educate the patients about the treatment and recruit them as collaborators. Each of the young adult patients in our pilot project were told that they were going to receive specialized trauma treatment. They were all introduced to the Structural Dissociation Model and asked if they thought it explained any of their difficulties. Almost immediately, most recognized the signs of the parts as very familiar to them. They could identify that their cry-for-help parts were triggered by staff hostility and frustration. They could see how their fight parts would respond by attacking their own bodies or assaulting staff. They described the hopelessness of their submit parts when it was apparent that staff were disappointed in them.

As the staff members involved in the pilot study began to speak the language of parts and helped their patients notice when they were triggered, these patients began to improve, some slightly and some dramatically. Noticing the impulse to self-harm as a fight part or a self-harming part allowed them to separate from the impulse. "That's the fight part, and I don't have to do what it wants," they would say. As the patients could increasingly differentiate their parts, they also became more aware of having a "Normal Life" self, despite having never experienced *normal* most of their lives. "That's the part of me that wants to go to college and get a good job," one might say. Another recognized it as "That's the part of me that wants a little home and a husband and kids." We found that their empathy and respect for the fight part's role in their survival seemed to settle this part down so that it was less reactive and impulsive. Protectiveness and kindness toward their attach and submit parts diminished the intensity of their hurt, shame, and anxious dependency on staff members.

When the Connecticut Department of Mental Health asked us for the name of this innovative treatment, I called it *Trauma-Informed Stabilization Treatment*. We needed to convince a government department that this treatment was sound and credible. To call it a parts treatment or a treatment for dissociation would have made it sound less credible. Trauma-Informed Stabilization Treatment (or TIST for short) communicated that this was a model that met the needs of the organization as well as the needs of the patients. It did not occur to me that TIST as a name failed to convey other important aspects of the treatment. It did not imply de-shaming people who felt worthless and disgusting. It did not convey the mindfulness-based nature of the approach or its self-compassion. And it did not convey the ultimate goal of TIST: to resolve the injuries of the past by facilitating healing relationships with the patients' most wounded parts.

## The Structure of the Treatment Program

This workbook will lead you through the various stages of the TIST model, guiding you through the healing process, one chapter at a time. It is intended for individuals who have survived trauma, as well as the therapists who support them. Whether you grew up in an abusive environment or experienced trauma as an adult (e.g., domestic violence, combat, racial trauma), the concepts in this book will help you understand and work with the effects of being traumatized. Even when your traumatic events have been acknowledged, their impact may still cause you to struggle day after day.

Being heard and acknowledged is a longed-for experience of traumatized individuals, so when parts are acknowledged, they feel some relief. With or without therapist support, you, too, can learn to identify distressing feelings as communications from your parts. As you learn to name what the parts are communicating, they will feel listened to, perhaps for the first time.

The first section of this book, chapters 1, 2, and 3, focuses on understanding the neurobiological foundation of this treatment model, helping you understand the process of fragmentation and how parts develop. You will also learn some basic skills that help set the stage for the work that follows.

Chapter 1 addresses how dissociation and fragmentation are normal responses to trauma that are not recognized as often as survivors need and deserve. You will learn the basic neurobiological processes that take place during trauma, as well as how and why you are triggered by reminders of the trauma. Recognizing your own fragmentation as a brilliant adaptation to an inescapably unsafe environment will help you appreciate your difficulties and symptoms as efforts to help you survive.

Chapter 2 focuses on ways to recognize the signs of being fragmented and, most importantly, appreciate the parts as they are triggered in your day-to-day life. You will start becoming familiar with your uniquely adapted parts and their role in your survival.

Having learned to recognize the parts, what do you do with them? In chapter 3, you will learn simple techniques for relating to your parts rather than becoming overwhelmed by their intense feelings and reactions. You will start by learning to notice distressing emotions and impulses as the feelings of parts. Rather than reacting to these feelings, you will learn to name them as the reactions of a part to some trigger or stress. We are used to thinking of ourselves as an *I*, but that often causes us to miss the cries for help or the protective efforts of our parts. You will learn to become fluent in the language of parts so that using the word part becomes automatic. Each time you say, "A part of me feels ____," rather than "I feel ____," the parts experience the sense of being recognized and visible.

Section 2 includes the next two chapters and focuses on how to change the relationship with your parts by developing awareness, building trust, and learning to communicate with the parts. There is no scientific test for parts, and sometimes it is difficult to differentiate ourselves from our parts when their feelings flood our bodies. When their trauma responses shut down your ability to think or notice, parts can take over, and your actions and reactions may begin to reflect their fears and needs.

Chapter 4 addresses this challenge. Once you can speak the language of parts, it will help you recognize *blending* (Schwartz & Sweezey, 2020), the experience of being so flooded with the feelings and point of view of a part that you lose awareness of the facts of your current life and your point of view. It is only by *unblending* from their overwhelming feelings that you and the part can be in relationship with each other. You can appreciate the part better when you are unblended, and the part experiences the felt sense of being seen. For our hospital patients, unblending allowed them to stabilize and begin to have a more stable sense of self.

Chapter 5 addresses the question of building trusting relationships with parts. How do we befriend them rather than ignore them or reject them? They have been ignored. They have been rejected. They have been unheard. How do we change that pattern? Learning to communicate and engage in dialogue is essential to trust in anyone. We can't heal parts with whom we have not developed trust or communication.

The next two chapters form Section 3 and will help you to delve deeper into understanding the complex impact of attachment trauma and to explore some of its most complicated aspects.

Chapter 6 focuses on the special challenges posed by traumatic attachment. Most child abuse happens at the hands of attachment figures, people to whom we are connected. Children's instinct to seek a parent when distressed or frightened is intense, but so also are the defensive responses of fight and flight. For traumatized children, the struggle is overwhelming because both instincts are stimulated by threat and danger. Fragmentation is doubly necessary in traumatic attachment.

Chapter 7 addresses the relationship between traumatized parts and self-destructive patterns, just as we did in developing the original TIST model. You may not have such extreme responses as did our state hospital patients, but you might recognize some self-destructive parts in yourself. In this chapter, we will explore how to identify these parts and how to understand their intentions, not just their behavior. Understanding them as protectors transforms your relationship to such parts and helps them to know you as trustworthy.

Section 4 focuses on repair. Chapter 8 will teach you ways to provide your parts with reparative experiences that disconfirm their deepest fears and soothe their hurt. Notice that healing is not equated with processing traumatic events in this model. The events are over, but what is not over is the suffering held by the parts. You can't cure their suffering by reliving the events. You must address their wounds and know how to repair them.

And finally, in chapter 9, you will explore what it is like to embrace yourself, to feel attached to every part of yourself. You may like or approve of some parts more than others, but embracing them implies that you equally accept and cherish the good, the bad, and the ugly. Through this process, you will find yourself appreciating even your darkest parts and caring deeply about how they feel even if you can't yet care about *them*. That is secure attachment, and it is yours no matter how traumatic your past may have been.

Let us start our TIST journey.

SECTION 1

# ESTABLISHING THE FOUNDATION:

## Understanding Fragmentation and Developing the Ability to Recognize Parts

CHAPTER 1

# Understanding How We Become Fragmented

Traumatic events rarely occur as single experiences. For most human beings, trauma occurs in a threatening, dangerous *environment.* Childhood abuse happens in abusive or neglectful families, domestic violence in the context of unsafe intimate partner relationships, war-related trauma in the context of military violence. Not only are the events overwhelming, but so is every hour of every day. The fear of what might happen is as bad as what actually does happen.

In the face of traumatic events, our minds need enough psychological distance from the fear and horror to remain emotionally intact. That distance is made possible by the mental ability of dissociation. As a mental ability, dissociation can also serve adaptive purposes beyond trauma: It supports peak performance in athletes, actors, and musicians by narrowing focus and muting distraction, and it enables health and emergency responders to remain calm and able to function effectively in high-stress situations.

## The Protective Role of Dissociation

In trauma, dissociation creates a sense of detachment from the traumatic experience, allowing our minds to watch what is occurring to us as if we were watching a movie. Many survivors describe floating up to the ceiling and observing the experience of being humiliated and abused as if it were happening to another person, a *bad* person, a person who is *not me.* Though it can be deeply disturbing to watch, by doing so from a distance, victims are left with a sense of being untouched by the abuse or the violence, thus being able to experience themselves as *good,* instead of damaged, preserving hope for the future. Splitting or fragmenting in this way becomes an ingenious and adaptive mental ability in a dangerous world.

However, the repeated, daily need to rely on dissociative disconnection to survive a traumatic environment and anticipate threat often results in the development of a fragmented personality system. Who *we* are becomes a system of parts adapted for surviving danger. In abusive environments, the traumatized parts of us quickly learn that it's safer to anticipate the next unsafe event than to dwell on what has already happened.

However, this adaptation has a steep price. To protect the *good* part of us, the mind pushes the rejected *not me* part out of consciousness and into the shadows, continuing to rely on dissociation, denial, and self-rejection to keep it hidden. Now, while the *good* self can be free to develop normally, the *bad* part waits in fear of whatever abuses or abandonments are about to happen next. In the end, we survive the failure of safety at the cost of disowning the wounded parts of who we are.

In addition, because we don't know that splitting will help us survive one day, we cannot appreciate that it is an ability to be able to go on as if nothing has happened. Instead, even as children, we can feel fraudulent. As we struggle to stay away from the *bad* side and identify with the good side, we have a felt sense of faking it, pretending, or putting on an act. Often, this conviction of fraudulence engenders painful self-doubt. Being able to go on with life becomes something shameful, rather than being understood as an act of courage and survival.

## How Trauma Is Stored in the Brain: The Living Legacy

The ability to stay conscious and present to witness what is happening is a luxury when we are in immediate danger. Faced with threat, the brain and body instinctively mobilize to act and protect us through the different defensive systems available to us: fighting, fleeing, ducking, hiding. As we sense danger cues, a chain reaction of neurochemical events is set in motion in the brain.

First, the *amygdala,* the brain's fire alarm and smoke detector, begins to fire more rapidly, turning on the sympathetic nervous system by releasing adrenaline. Adrenaline speeds up our heart rate and breathing to increase oxygen flow to muscle tissue. Our bodies are now energized for action.

The prefrontal cortex (the Thinking Brain) shuts down to facilitate instinctive responding. The events unfold in slow motion; an icy calm replaces fear; the eyes narrow; and the body prepares for action, clenching our fists and engaging our leg, arm, and shoulder muscles. As the body prepares to fight or flee, the parasympathetic nervous system comes online, preparing us to submit if there is no way out and no way to defend. The parasympathetic system also helps the body recover from the massive expenditure of energy involved in fighting or fleeing. Rather than feeling relief or being able to rest after it is over, we feel depleted, exhausted, and numb.

When the autonomic nervous system is activated by traumatic threats, another important part of the brain is inhibited. The *hippocampus,* the part of the brain responsible for organizing experiences into chronological order so that they can be put into words, is suppressed. Without either a functioning hippocampus or a prefrontal cortex, we are deprived of the opportunity to process the event and are left instead with only "the sensory elements of [the] experience unintegrated and unattached" (van der Kolk et al., 2001, p. 18). For the very worst events, the brain's survival responses prevent the mind and body from making meaning of what has happened. We are left with a confusing array of overwhelming feelings, frightening images, and physical reactions without words—all unrecognizable as *memory*.

How each person encodes memories of their traumatic past is unique and different, but what everyone has in common is the way that traumatic memory is fragmented and unintegrated. Brain scan research over the past 30 years reveals that what the human brain *remembers* after trauma is more likely to be single images, strong emotions, or physical reactions rather than narrative memories that make a clearcut case for what happened "beyond a reasonable doubt" (Perl et al., 2023; van der Kolk, 2014). Some trauma survivors have explicit memories of events; some have little to none. All have a host of implicit memories, including trauma-related emotions, autonomic arousal responses, muscle and body memories, visceral memories, as well as tactile-olfactory-visual and auditory memories. This is what we call *the living legacy of trauma* (Fisher, 2021): nonverbal, emotional, and sensory memory without a context, which are held by different fragmented parts or selves. In addition, we also have symptoms or difficulties that reflect how we have adapted to the unsafe conditions we faced. Hopelessness is adaptive when hope always leads to disappointment or exploitation. Sleeplessness is protective when we are likely to be woken suddenly and abused in the middle of the night.

## Remembering Actions and Reactions

As a preventive measure, the human brain has a negativity bias that makes us especially sensitive to all the people, places, and things that are related to previous danger. When we perceive triggering people or situations as unsafe, we tend to associate those triggers with danger or menace. Once something becomes a trigger, the body and the parts respond to it as if it's a danger signal in its own right, stimulating uninvited, implicit memories. The brain circuits described above turn on again: The amygdala is unable to distinguish between real or perceived danger, and it fires its alarm signal; the Thinking Brain shuts down; and there is no mindful Noticing Brain to help us discriminate feeling memories from present reality. We feel unsafe even in the safest of environments.

> To help you understand how your current symptoms and difficulties may have helped you and your parts to survive, take a look at **Worksheet 1a**, ***The Signs of Trauma***. Be curious. Don't add your symptoms up and judge yourself. These symptoms tell the story of how your mind and body adapted to a threatening world. They are a testimony of survival. Use **Worksheet 1b** to notice how your most distressing issues or symptoms helped you survive. How does that change how you view them?

For survivors of trauma that happened long ago, this reactivation of memory via triggers is especially costly. Many people are victims of triggering for many more years than they were victims of traumatic events. Survivors of trauma report feeling anxious, depressed, sad, lonely, alienated, or angry. They are often troubled by fear, dread, chronic shame, self-hatred, a conviction that the worst is about to happen, hopelessness, helplessness, fear of abandonment, numbing, and disconnection from emotions. All these symptoms can represent feeling and body memories (Damis, 2022), but we have no idea that we are remembering. How could we? We experience the feelings unrelated to any context other than the present moment. Not only are we unaware of the parts, but we are also unaware that what we feel tells us what the parts are remembering. Without awareness that our triggered responses are evidence of body and emotional memory held by parts, it is easy to believe the pounding heartbeat, burning shame, inability to breathe, numbing, or rage are signs that we are in danger right now.

When it becomes clear that we are not at risk, other fears arise: *Maybe I am going crazy, or am I just pretending?* On the basis of what feels like compelling evidence, and not knowing that we are triggered, it is natural to isolate and withdraw, end healthy relationships prematurely or explosively, or lose the ability to end unhealthy ones. Many of us continue to function, but we avoid living life fully to reduce the exposure to triggers. Others (like the state hospital patients) engage in self-destructive behavior to manage their overwhelming feelings and activation, leaving them feeling even more damaged and defective.

In traumatic environments where the threat of danger was ever-present, our brains and bodies became conditioned to maintain a readiness for potential threat. In some environments, it is safer to have sympathetically activated responses (hypervigilance, high arousal, readiness to take action, impulsivity) and, in others, it is more adaptive to become parasympathetically dominant (no energy, exhausted, slowed, numb, hopeless, helpless). For children or victims of domestic violence who endure 24-hour conditions of threat each day, or for whom being seen and not heard is the safest adaptation, parasympathetic patterns become automatic. Passivity, slowed thinking, depression, or shame dominate the individual's experience. In sympathetically dominant survivors, it is more typical to see mistrust, hypervigilance, feelings of anger or fear, and impulsivity. Though the events may have happened years ago, these adaptations persist either chronically or when we encounter certain triggers.

## The Process of Becoming Fragmented

As you saw in the beginning of the chapter, it is easy and instinctive for our brains to split or fragment. What we call *the brain* is composed of many separate structures serving different functions that coordinate and communicate via neural pathways. The Structural Dissociation Model (van der Hart et al., 2006) emphasizes this fact: We are all born with brains that are physically split. The biggest *fault line* in the brain is between the left and right hemispheres, the two sides of the brain. Each side is very different in what it offers us. We are right-brain dominant for most of childhood, reliant on a hemisphere that has no verbal language but is good at understanding body language, emotion, and intuition. The slower developing left brain has very different abilities: It speaks in words, can organize ideas, learns from past experience, problem solves, and sees the big picture. It develops very gradually over the course of the first 18 years of life. We don't consistently begin to think and remember in words until we reach the ages of 9 or 10. We remember early childhood with our right brains, without words. Development of the prefrontal cortex—the most advanced region of the brain—continues throughout adolescence and early adulthood, up until the age of 30. That includes the right prefrontal cortex (the Feeling Brain), the left prefrontal cortex (the Thinking Brain), and the medial prefrontal cortex in the middle of the forehead (the Noticing Brain).

In the early years of childhood, right and left brains operate relatively independently of each other. The ability for the two sides to communicate is dependent on a yet another region called the *corpus callosum*, a long thin structure that only becomes fully developed around the age of 12 and is less well-developed in traumatized children and adolescents.

In unsafe environments, both sides of the brain are necessary in response to changing moment-to-moment conditions. For example, going to school requires a left-brain part of the personality that can pay attention in class, learn new information, and socially engage with peers and teachers. At home, with parents who may be neglectful at certain times and violent at others, the ability to rapidly shift from one emotional or body state to another could be essential. Fear could alert us to danger in response to the sound of our parents' voice or footsteps. Playfulness could lift our parents' irritable mood and make them laugh. The submission response could help us become precociously compliant to avoid conflict. At other times, it might be safest to stay quietly on guard, carefully observing our parents' mood and reacting in whatever ways best defend against their abusive behavior.

In summary, in a complicated and unsafe environment, adaptation favors the development of a fluid system of selves rather than one fully integrated *self*. Week after week, year after year, traumatized individuals survive a threatening world thanks to the parts that vigilantly anticipate and respond to danger. How aware they are of their parts is dependent on what is most adaptive.

## Conclusion

Understanding how we become fragmented is central to understanding how we survive trauma. This chapter has explored the instinctive, adaptive brilliance of dissociation and fragmentation—not as signs of weakness or pathology, but as a heroic survival strategy developed in response to overwhelming environments. The capacity to split into parts allows the mind to preserve a sense of goodness, agency, and hope, even when the parts convey shame, hopelessness, and fear. These parts, each aligned with fundamental survival responses, form a fluid internal system that enables children and adults alike to navigate unsafe worlds. But while this fragmentation protects us, it also comes at the cost of internal alienation, chronic dysregulation, and the loss of a coherent narrative memory.

Trauma leaves behind a legacy that is stored not in words, but in emotions, bodily sensations, impulses, and internal conflicts—often unrecognized as memories at all. The trauma-related parts continue to respond as if the danger is still present, even when life circumstances have changed. The emotional and physical responses they carry can dominate our daily lives, creating confusion, shame, and despair. Recognizing these symptoms as messages from dissociated parts offers a path to healing. Understanding the fragmentation that once ensured survival becomes an invitation to reweave a more compassionate and cohesive sense of self.

As you will see in the next chapter, we can live a normal life after trauma, but we cannot leave our parts behind. Having been traumatized in the course of daily life, the parts eventually will be triggered by cues both stressful and benign, both big and small, which are connected to the trauma.

Worksheet 1a

# The Signs of Trauma

Circle the symptoms and difficulties you recognize as familiar. Put a check mark next to those you never knew were the result of your trauma!

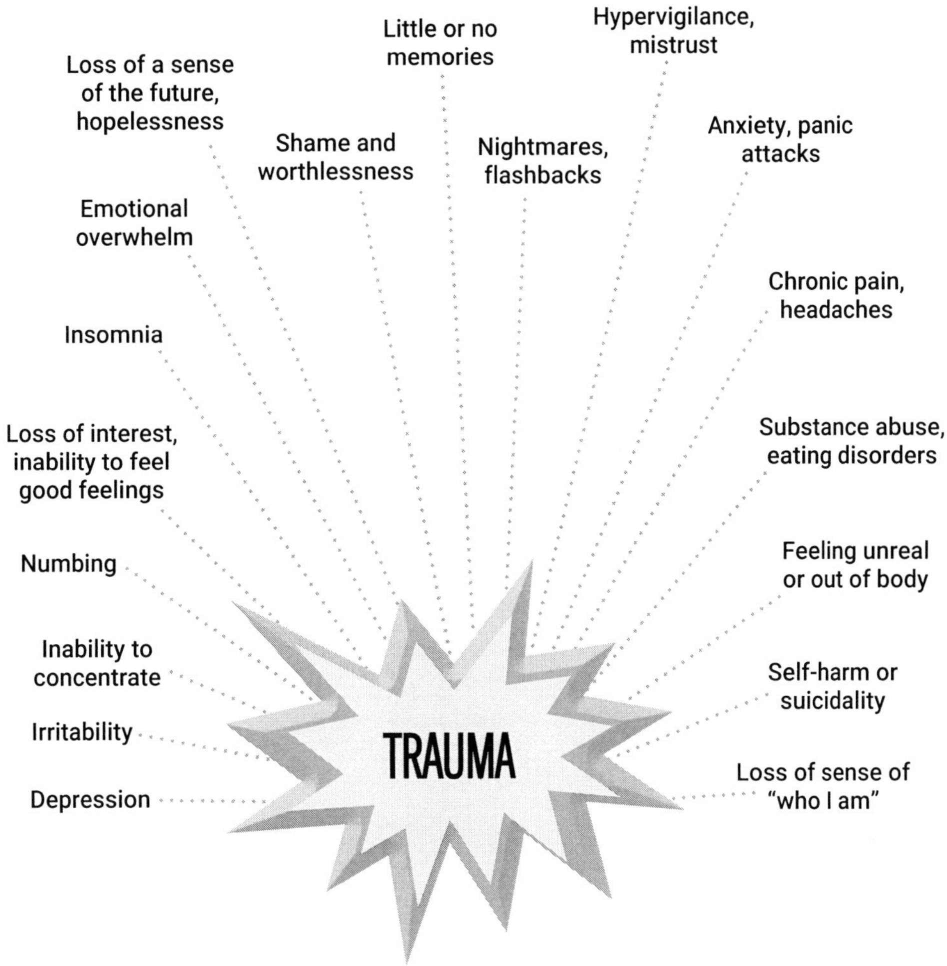


How do your feelings about yourself change when you see that these problems or symptoms are part of the living legacy of the trauma?

________________________________________________

________________________________________________

________________________________________________

________________________________________________

Worksheet 1b

# How Did Your Symptoms Help You Survive?

Choose four of your most troubling or difficult feelings or issues, and then ask yourself: "How did this help me survive? How did it help me get through?" (e.g., How did losing interest in things help me? How did not sleeping help? How did it help to want to die? )

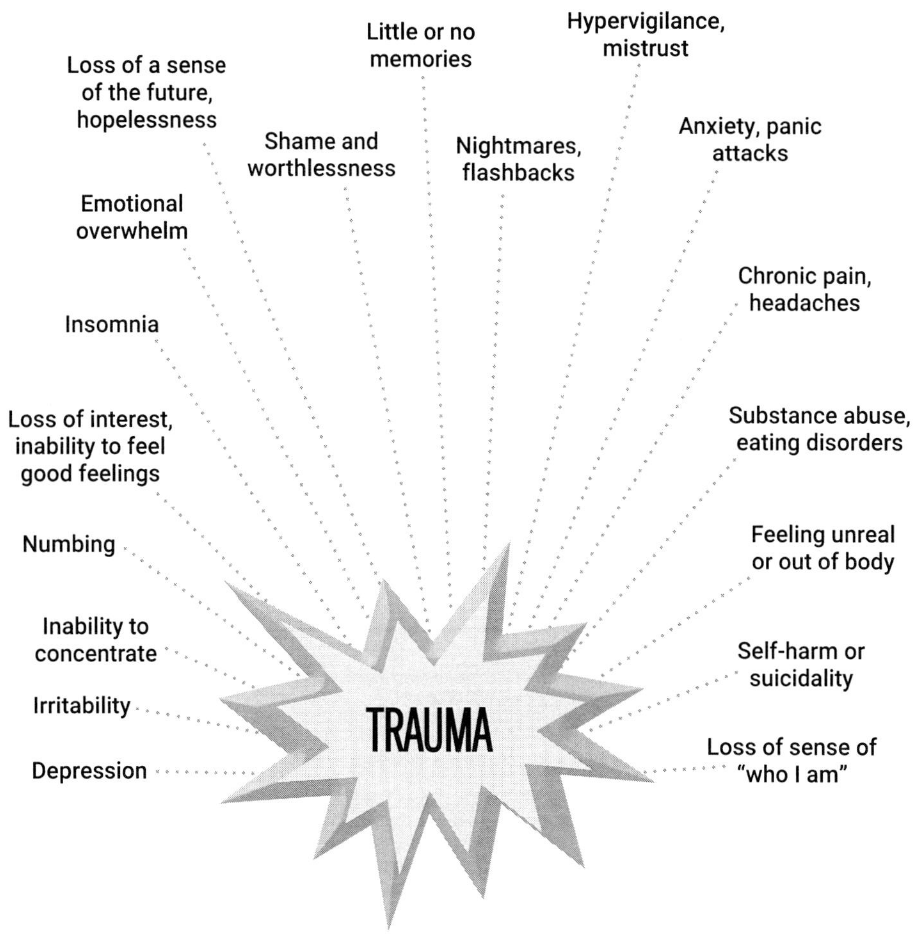


Write in whatever you discover below. If you are unsure of an answer, ask yourself, "What would it have been like if I *hadn't* had this reaction?"

1. ______________________________

2. ______________________________

3. ______________________________

4. ______________________________

CHAPTER 2

# Recognizing Our Parts in Daily Life

Because this system of selves continues to anticipate threat and affect our present reality, it is more helpful to begin learning how to recognize these parts rather than try to ignore them.

## How Having Parts Supports Survival

When there are signs of immediate threat, the nervous system instinctively mobilizes whatever part whose response is considered most adaptive in that moment in that particular environment. Think about these phrases as they apply to your experience: If you recall, "I had to be seen and not heard," you are describing a part that could be still and silent. If you remember, "I always had to have eyes in the back of my head," you are talking about a watchful, vigilant fight part. "I tried to get people to like me" suggests a cry-for-help part trying to elicit protection and validation. "I survived my childhood by hiding behind the sofa" describes a fear or freeze part who learned how to be invisible. "I learned to run and hide before he could get to me" suggests a flight part that was instrumental to your survival in a threatening world.

Connecting different parts to their survival responses often diminishes the shame and self-doubt you might feel. The fear of abandonment is understandable when you notice it as the fear of the cry-for-help or attach part. Experiences where you felt rage make more sense when you understand them as a fight part triggered by unfairness or bad behavior. The inability to say "no" or to have a voice feels less shameful when you connect it to a young submissive part whose sense of safety is tied to pleasing others.

The concept that each part represents a way of surviving dangerous conditions, that each part represents a different approach to self-protection, gives meaning and dignity to the fragmentation. The parts in this view are not time capsules of memory. They are the heroes of our stories—a means of surviving the worst of the worst, not a means of remembering it. They just don't know that the war is over. As carriers of our instinctive survival responses, the parts remain poised for the next threat for decades after *it* is over.

## Recognizing the Signs of Structurally Dissociated Parts

In the Structural Dissociation Model, the part of us that is driven by left-brain-related priorities is labeled the *Apparently Normal Part of the Personality*, and the parts that are driven by right-brain survival responses are called the *Emotional Parts of the Personality*. In this book, I will use terms that honor how the parts helped us survive: The left-brain part of the personality is termed the *Going On with Normal Life* part, and the right-brain parts are the *trauma-related* parts. By avoiding the words *apparently normal*, my goal is to challenge our tendencies to see the ability to function as a *false self*. If we do that, then the *true self* consists only of trauma-related parts. And if that is the case, who will be left to help them?

Typically, while the Going On with Normal Life part is trying to carry on (functioning at a job, raising children, organizing home life, taking up meaningful personal and professional goals), the trauma-related parts (fight, flight, freeze, submit, and cling or attach for survival) continue to be triggered by ordinary experiences. Their constant hypervigilance and mistrust, overwhelming emotions, incapacitating depression or anxiety, self-destructive behavior, and fear or hopelessness about the future make it harder to keep going.

Using the Structural Dissociation Model is helpful because it provides a scientifically informed explanation and offers a map to understanding ourselves. Ask yourself, "Do I recognize any of these parts in myself? Do any of them seem familiar?"

> This might be a good point at which to look at **Worksheet 2** and see if you recognize any signs of the Going On with Normal Life part in yourself and any signs of the trauma-related parts of your personality. How does it change how you think about yourself when you look at the division inside you as a survival strategy?

## How Can You Tell If You Are Fragmented?

There are certain symptoms that can alert you to the presence of fragmented parts. For example:

- **Signs of internal splitting:** You function highly at work where there are positive triggers (work assignments, responsibilities) but find yourself triggered in personal relationships. Or you experience fears of abandonment that alternate with attempts to push away those who try to get close. Or you tend to initially trust others before you really know them, followed by disillusionment and anger when those individuals fail you. Or you have contradictory reactions: For example, you might feel intense fear around certain triggers but forget to be careful about actual threats, like not wearing a seatbelt or not locking the door. You plan a long-awaited family vacation for the following summer, but all the while, you can't stop thinking about wanting to die.

- **Treatment history:** You have had several previous treatments for the same symptoms that have resulted in little progress or clarity. Or perhaps your therapy experiences were rocky and tumultuous or were ended precipitously by either you or the therapist. Your therapist might have expressed, "I don't have the skills you need" or "It's not a good fit," leaving you feeling abandoned or threatened with abandonment. If you are one of the many survivors who fear a therapist's abandonment more than any lack of skill, each failed treatment communicates, "You're too difficult to be treated," "Something is wrong with you," or "I can't be there for you."

- **Somatic symptoms:** Unusual pain sensitivity or uncharacteristically high pain tolerance, stress-related headaches, eye blinking or drooping, and even physical symptoms with no diagnosable medical cause can often be parts-related. One of the most common indicators of structural dissociation is an atypical response or non-responsiveness to psychiatric medications.

- **Behavior or thinking that suggests child parts:** Another sign of fragmented parts is the presence of childlike body language. You might come across as shy, collapsed, fearful, unable to tolerate being seen, or unable to make eye contact. In many normal interpersonal situations, you might think, "I'm scared—don't hurt me," "Please like me," or "Please don't leave me." Other signs of child parts include concrete thinking; worries about separation, caring, and fairness; and feeling hurt when other people are not warm and understanding. You might even judge yourself as "acting like a baby," not knowing that you are experiencing the feelings of a very young part.

- **Patterns of indecision or self-sabotage**: Often misinterpreted as ambivalence, the inability to make small, everyday decisions or carry out your goals can reflect conflicts between parts with opposite aims. Often, this manifests as frequent job, career, or relationship changes, or a history of successes in life that alternate with self-sabotage or failure. Very crucial life decisions can be involved, but this pattern can also appear in everyday ways, such as the inability to choose what to wear in the morning, what to eat for breakfast, and whether to keep a date with a friend for lunch.

Then turn to **Worksheet 3** and see if you recognize any of the trauma-related parts inside you. Do any of these parts resonate with you? Don't worry if you don't have all of them or are not sure. Look for familiarity. For example, "I always tell myself I'm not going to yell at my children today, and then it just happens." Ask yourself: "Do I have a part that always says yes when I want to say no? Do I have a part that's needy? Do I have a part that's ashamed or critical of the neediness?"

## Resolving Trauma by Working with Parts

Research on traumatic memory shows that when we are asked to remember a traumatic event, our instinctive emergency responses are stimulated as if the event were taking place all over again (van der Kolk, 2014). Remember that because of the amygdala's inability to distinguish true danger from perceived danger, the brain's prefrontal cortex (our Thinking Brain) reduces activity or shuts down, making it hard to think or put our feelings into words. No wonder survivors don't tell anyone what happened to them! Not only is it unsafe to tell, but our ability to speak is inhibited by the brain's responses to threat.

Once trauma was recognized decades ago for its psychological impact, therapists relied on the "talking cure," which has remained the most accepted practice in psychotherapy from the time of Freud to the present day. Therapists would help clients recall the traumatic events they remembered. But as clients tried to talk about what happened, the implicit feeling memories held by different parts became stimulated, and the client would feel overwhelmed rather than relieved. No one understood that the living legacy of trauma was at work. No one realized that traumatized parts were reactivated by the remembering, causing them to once again experience the feeling of struggling to survive. The *not me* parts were reliving the past and crying for help.

To recognize the signs of structural dissociation that might indicate the presence of a part, turn to **Worksheet 4**. Notice the signs that are familiar to you so you can recognize them as they occur.

That's why it's so important to begin trusting that your triggered states tell the story of the past, even if you can't recall—or would rather not recall—specific incidents. These emotional and physical reactions are memories in their own right, whether they are connected to a clear explicit memory or not. The body remembers implicitly what the mind cannot, and recognizing feeling memories will help you meet triggered experiences with less shame and more understanding.

While the body's drive to stay alert has helped us survive, that same vigilance can make it hard to recover. The instinct to prepare for the next threat interferes with our capacity to experience safety, calm, or a sense of "it's over now." Even years later, many trauma survivors find that the serenity they want can feel foreign or even threatening. Clients often report feeling uneasy in moments of peace: "It feels so weird," they'll say, "I'm not comfortable with it." This discomfort is not a failure—it's a legacy of the nervous system's enduring protection.

Years ago, we did not know that resolution of the past requires *transforming* the memories, not reliving them. The transformation of traumatic memory is facilitated by changes in our relationship to both implicit and explicit memories. This happens naturally and organically as you begin to notice triggered states as communications from parts. When you can connect feeling memory states to younger parts, it is easier to address them as a record of old dangers instead of signs of current threat. When the intense sensations, emotions, and images are treated as *their* feelings, it is easier to tolerate the intensity. Feeling compassion or protectiveness for our younger selves also helps us to feel our *bigness*—to appreciate our adult capabilities and resources and see the greater respect that we are accorded as adults, along with the greater safety it affords us in everyday life. When fear or shame is recognized as the feeling memory of a wounded part, it transforms our relationship to that feeling. Now, there is a suffering person whose emotions we can feel. And there is a *me* observing that part from the safety of the present moment.

## Conclusion

Recognizing our parts in daily life is the first step in transforming how we understand ourselves. What once felt like overwhelming emotion, self-sabotage, or shameful behavior can now be seen as the expression of parts that once protected us. These parts are not signs of weakness or brokenness; they are the embodied memories of how we survived. By learning to identify their signals—whether fear, indecision, physical symptoms, or sudden shifts in mood—we begin to interrupt the cycle of reactivity and open the door to healing with compassion and curiosity.

Understanding your inner world through the lens of parts allows you to respond to suffering from the wise, grounded presence of your adult self. You do not need to relive the pain to resolve it. Instead, by noticing and engaging with these inner states as communications from your traumatized selves, you reclaim the power to care for them from the safety of the present. This chapter is an invitation to look within not for what's wrong, but for who needs your help—and to realize that the one who can help is already here.

Worksheet 2

# The Structural Dissociation Model

**Pre-traumatic Personality**

How old were you when the first traumas happened?

______________________________

______________________________

______________________________

______________________________

**"Going On with Normal Life" Part of the Personality**

Describe some of the things you do that reflect this side of you—like taking care of your home, managing bills and chores, and so on.

______________________________

______________________________

______________________________

______________________________

______________________________

**Trauma-Related Parts of the Personality**

Describe what it is like when you are in this side of yourself—like being afraid or angry or not wanting to see anyone.

______________________________

______________________________

______________________________

______________________________

______________________________

Worksheet 3

# Identifying Your Traumatized Parts

Be curious about how these different types of parts are evident in your life. Write down the qualities or behaviors that you connect to with these different kinds of parts.

**"Going On with Normal Life" Part** — **Trauma-Related Parts**

| Fight Part | Flight Part | Freeze Part | Submit Part | Cry-for-Help Part |
|---|---|---|---|---|
| How do you recognize your fight part? | What signs of flight do you notice? | Is there a part that is fearful? | Is there a depressed or ashamed part? | Is there a sad, lonely, or needy part? |

Worksheet 4

# Signs of Structural Dissociation

You might notice different sides of you in the descriptions below. Put a check mark by any signs of structural dissociation that are familiar to you, and note which part the feeling or behavior might belong to:

- ☐ Able to function in some situations but not in others ______________
- ☐ Feel overwhelming emotions or no emotion at all ______________
- ☐ Have sudden, intense physical reactions ______________
- ☐ Often feel out of control regarding what I do and say ______________
- ☐ Anxiety rules my life ______________
- ☐ Feel "possessed" sometimes ______________
- ☐ Can't stop hurting myself ______________
- ☐ Can't stop drinking or drugging ______________
- ☐ Have plans for the future, but I don't want to live ______________
- ☐ Feel out of control of my body ______________
- ☐ Have trouble making decisions ______________
- ☐ Feel insecure about being accepted by others or about belonging ______________
- ☐ Either I can't trust anyone, or I trust too easily ______________
- ☐ Have fears of abandonment ______________
- ☐ Feel like "I'm all over the place" ______________
- ☐ Depression rules my life ______________
- ☐ Hate myself ______________
- ☐ Anger rules my life ______________
- ☐ Shame rules my life ______________
- ☐ Push other people away ______________
- ☐ Am too dependent, too needy ______________
- ☐ Don't know who I am anymore ______________
- ☐ Have trouble with my memory ______________

What changes when you think of these reactions as coming from different parts of you?

______________________________________________

______________________________________________

 

CHAPTER 3

# Befriending Our Parts Through Curiosity

As we saw in chapter 1, when traumatic events suddenly occur, and the prefrontal cortex shuts down, we lose our ability to put words to experience and emotion. The overwhelming feelings and physical reactions are too big to be captured by language. Afterward, we may try to describe the experience but can only approximate a "feeling of what happened" (Damasio, 1999), biased by whatever meaning-making we have attached to the event.

Often, our stories do not fully capture the details of the traumatic event itself but, rather, how each part experienced themselves as a result of it. Feeling ashamed, dirty or disgusting, or painfully exposed are not descriptions of an event; they convey the feeling memories still held by fragmented parts.

## Is Implicit Memory a Way to Help Us Remain Safe?

Research shows that even verbalized accounts of traumatic events are very different from the memories of sad, distressing events: "Traumatic memories are not experienced as memories as such. Rather, these are fragments of prior events, subjugating the present moment to evade the sense of belonging to the past" (Perl et al., 2023, p. 2235).

Why would our brains evade the sense of belonging to the past? Perhaps evolution taught the brain and body that it is safer for humans to experience the trauma as if it were *still a threat now* rather than experience it as a past event and let down our guard. Maybe that is why we remember trauma primarily through implicit memories. It helps us to stay vigilant long after the event is over.

When we start to understand traumatic memory from a parts perspective, we don't have to treat verbal memories as something to avoid or pursue. We are remembering all the time. The feelings and body memories of our parts, triggered by benign everyday experiences, repeatedly come alive in our bodies and minds. Consider Annie's story:

> *Annie felt anxious and overwhelmed every time she left the house to go to the grocery store. Her young parts were afraid of being unwelcome, and her protector parts saw it as too risky to go out into a dangerous world. But other parts were triggered when she didn't leave the house. Alone at home, they reexperienced the sense of isolation, not belonging, and painful loneliness of her childhood. While Annie continued to stay home alone—lonely and too defective to leave the house—her parts were reliving the emotional experience of her childhood. The past had not been left behind; the parts still relived it every day. It's not safe to be alone, it's not safe to be around people, it's not safe at home, and it's not safe to be outside the home. That is what they had learned.*

It took endless practice to notice these intense feelings and patterns of reaction as communications from Annie's parts rather than as the story of her life. She and her husband lived in a safe semi-rural community, not in the urban housing project where she grew up, but how would the parts have known that? The dissociative barriers between Annie and her parts ensured that they did not know, and she was not aware that they did not know. That was the price she had paid to survive. She was spared full awareness of the trauma, but the parts were deprived of any awareness of the safety she had fought so hard to achieve.

## The Importance of the Noticing Brain

Most of us are accustomed to using our Thinking Brains to ask, "Why am I feeling this way?" "Why am I being treated this way?" and "What do I do about this?" The left-hemisphere Thinking Brain is good at problem-solving, developing insight, remembering chronologically, holding information, and coming to conclusions. But to resolve trauma, we need the Noticing Brain. Located in the medial prefrontal cortex, just behind the center of your forehead, the Noticing Brain is very different from your Thinking Brain. It simply observes—with curiosity and interest, without judgment or opinion. It neither endorses nor rejects whatever we notice. If we do have a reaction coming from other parts of the brain, that, too, can be noticed. The Noticing Brain remains neutral, simply acknowledging what's happening with a mindful attitude of: "It is what it is." And because the Noticing Brain is connected to the amygdala, the more active the Noticing Brain becomes, the calmer the amygdala.

## Assume Distress Is a Communication from a Part

Resolving a traumatic past implies that we must first change the story of our current lives. Without acknowledging the fragmentation or the parts, we see only one aspect of ourselves. It is easy to become chronically depressed or angry or hopeless when we do not see the role of the parts in the distress we feel. It is easy to believe we are worthless, undeserving, and inadequate when we don't know that these beliefs are communications from parts who were made to feel less than others.

Take a leap of faith.

Assume that any distressing feelings you experience are communications from parts. Of course, that does not mean your Going On with Normal Life part has never had distressing feelings in response to major loss, stress, or rejection. But generally, when bad things happen to us as adults, we have a mixture of feelings, and we can manage our emotions with creativity and resilience. The distressing feelings of the parts are triggered by benign or moderately stressful events; they are intense; and, most of all, they usually feel familiar.

*Annie's child parts were triggered daily by her very quiet, taciturn husband. To these parts, his reserve seemed intentional, and they felt rejected and unimportant to him. The child parts' distress would then trigger angry parts who would threaten to leave him or would shame him. He would become even quieter, afraid to provoke the angry parts. And then both the hurt and angry parts would feel confirmed in their judgment of him.*

*Years later, when Annie could see her husband from a Noticing Brain perspective, she could appreciate that his reserve had nothing to do with her personally, and she could recognize the nonverbal ways he communicated his love and commitment to her.*

To become aware of and familiar with the role of our parts in our emotional and relational lives requires that we notice them. Each time you think, "I'm depressed" or "I'm anxious," pause for a moment and notice that feeling of depression or anxiety as a part. Observe that a part of you is anxious or a part of you is depressed, not the whole you.

Be curious—this part is trying to communicate to you. It wants someone to know that it's anxious. In mindfulness language, we simply describe what we notice: "The anxious part gets anxious each time a thought comes up about my job interview." That simple description acknowledges the part and communicates, "I hear you." Learning to mindfully notice our distressing feelings as *parts* changes our relationship to them and the emotions they carry. It takes practice to observe rather than react to what we feel, but the reward is that we and they feel more relief.

Turn to **Worksheet 5, *Identifying Parts***. This worksheet will help you recognize the subtle signs of different parts as they are triggered throughout the course of a day. Although each is driven by a survival response, they can only be identified by their feelings and behaviors.

## Speak the Language of Parts

When we acknowledge communications from parts in the form of distressing, uncomfortable thoughts and feelings, we begin to build a relationship with them. Validating that these parts come from an unsafe world—without having to explore all the details—is reassuring to them. Their experience was that no one saw or understood what was happening to them. They don't need to share the details. They just need someone to know that they still don't feel safe. Matter-of-fact acknowledgment of the traumatic past often calms the parts rather than activating them. It conveys, "Someone knows how it was."

To resolve trauma, we have to develop a relationship to parts holding the felt experience of an unsafe world. The longing to be heard is a natural human response to feeling unsafe or abandoned, or to having to keep terrible secrets. Few people can safely tell their story to anyone at the time of the abuse, leaving behind a feeling memory of a longing to tell that was never satisfied.

Now there is someone to tell: you. But how will the parts know that you hear them unless you use the language of parts? This is a foreign language for most of us. We grew up saying, "I feel" and "I think." Although we might use the word *part* in casual conversation to talk about inner conflicts, we actually don't think of ourselves as fragmented. But to help our parts heal and recover, it's a language we must speak.

We must move from an "I" narrative to a parts narrative. Whether the story we have told ourselves is "I've gotten over it," "I am worthless and irreparably damaged," or "I am a proud survivor," looking at our story from an "I" perspective doesn't do the parts justice. We must replace the habitual "I feel . . ." with the unfamiliar "A part of me feels . . ." Think of it as speaking *their* language.

In any language learning, consistency is important: If we are taking a Spanish class, we need to speak Spanish to become fluent. This is equally true with parts language. Assume that distressing feelings are cries from parts. Noticing them and acknowledging their presence requires us to use their language. Otherwise, they will not know they are being heard.

**Worksheet 6** is about the language of parts. Practice translating your "I" statements into parts language. Think of it as a language class handout. You need practice to become fluent in a new language.

## Validate and Relate to Parts with Compassion

As we learn to mindfully notice the distress of our wounded parts and understand it as their pain, we also need to validate each part. This is not always an easy step for those of us whose way of distancing ourselves from the *not me* parts has been to loathe and despise their feelings. To be able to validate a part, we have to pause and be curious about the part who is afraid, ashamed, or hurt and lonely.

Try to sense how old the part is by how it speaks, thinks, or feels. Does it sound like a very young child? A three- or four-year-old? Or more like a slightly older child who's nine or ten? A teenager or young adult? Don't try to estimate its age by remembering events or trying to visualize the part. If you think of the part as emerging in the context of some specific experience, you may fail to recognize that it is now at an older age and has been impacted by many events.

Day after day, as troubling issues or distressing feelings arise, continue to notice which part is upset and what has triggered that part. The assumption that every feeling of upset is always a communication from a part is not a scientific fact, of course. It represents a way of relating to our emotions and our parts in a mindful, compassionate, non-pathologizing way.

Underlying these assumptions is a mindfulness-related belief that when we notice thoughts, feelings, and body experiences with interest, curiosity, and compassion, it is likely to lead to a positive change in our state of mind. If you consistently take a mental step back, increase your curiosity about part(s) who are having a hard time, notice the bodily and emotional signs that communicate their feelings, and then experiment with what might help the parts feel heard, you will be processing posttraumatic memory. Through this simple act of noticing and assigning distressing feelings to younger selves, you can learn to feel less afraid of your triggered responses and more connected to and protective of your parts, rather than ashamed of and alienated from them.

## Conclusion

In TIST, the focus is not on traumatic events but on the *legacy of trauma* as it is carried by the parts—a legacy that continues to intrude into our minds and bodies even decades later. *Processing the trauma* in TIST means *transforming* how the parts have encoded the effects of the traumatic events by transforming our relationship with these parts. It entails a shift from alienation to unconditional acceptance and attachment repair.

If you have had months or years of event-focused trauma treatment, it can be hard to shift from a narrative approach to a *repair* perspective. What you need to remember is that the early trauma treatment field's focus on events simply reflected how little the mental health world knew about trauma. We believed that putting these events into words would lay the memories to rest and that we would no longer suffer their effects. Decades later, we have a very different understanding of traumatization and how to treat it. Most experts now realize that healing and repair are not so simple.

Remembering the past is helpful only to the extent that it helps to heal rather than reopen the wounds. Memory work should never be used in the service of reliving your painful past or asking your parts to relive it. Remembering should serve a larger purpose: to change the ending to every part's story until each one feels safe. Remembrance should be used as a catalyst to evoke a deeper appreciation for how we survived with heart and soul intact, and gratitude for all the parts who helped ensure survival and now deserve to be part of a safe and healthy present.

Worksheet 5

# Identifying Parts

Circle the qualities of each part that you recognize in yourself. What changes when you identify depressed feelings as a depressed part? Or angry feelings as an angry part?

**"Going On with Normal Life" Part** — **Trauma-Related Parts**

| **Fight Part**<br>Vigilance | **Flight Part**<br>Escape | **Freeze Part**<br>Fear | **Submit Part**<br>Shame | **Cry-for-Help Part**<br>Needy |
|---|---|---|---|---|
| Angry | Distancer | Frozen | Depressed | Desperate |
| Judgmental | Ambivalent | Terrified | Ashamed | Craves connection |
| Suspicious | Cannot commit | Wary | Filled with self-hatred | Innocent |
| Mistrustful | Addictive or eating-disordered behavior | Phobic of being seen | Passive | Trusting |
| Self-destructive | | Panic attacks | Tries to be good | Wants to be liked |
| Suicidal | | Nightmares | Caretaker | Wants someone to care |
| Needs to control | | Flashbacks | Self-sacrificing | |

Worksheet 6

# Using Parts Language

It takes practice to translate what you feel into parts language. Take each feeling below and see what happens if you translate it into parts language.

I feel shaky. ⟶ ________________________________

I feel very ashamed. ⟶ ________________________________

I don't want to stop drinking. ⟶ ________________________________

I hate myself. ⟶ ________________________________

I feel nervous. ⟶ ________________________________

Anger rules my life. ⟶ ________________________________

I can't stop hurting myself. ⟶ ________________________________

I have plans for the future, but I don't want to live. ⟶ ________________________________

I want closeness, but I avoid people. ⟶ ________________________________

I feel defective. ⟶ ________________________________

I just want to give up. ⟶ ________________________________

What feels different when you use the language of parts?

________________________________________________________________

________________________________________________________________

________________________________________________________________

SECTION 2

# DEVELOPING RELATIONSHIP:

## Building Awareness, Trust, and Communication with Our Parts

CHAPTER 4

# Unblending: Staying Present While Parts Are Activated

In a traumatic environment, even when the only option is to feign death (e.g., go numb, pretend to be asleep, imagine floating up to the ceiling), the body instinctively chooses the defensive response most likely to succeed in limiting the injury, shock, or pain. When we freeze in fear, inhibit our active defenses, or can't speak, it is adaptive. After all, what could we say that wouldn't provoke the abuser? In contrast, when we do fight back, even if it's a losing battle, our survival defense system has instinctively assessed that, in *this* situation, it is safer to fight than to submit, even though resistance may result in punishment. These survival responses become automatic over time—even years later.

Naming distress as a part tells our parts that we're listening, that they are seen and heard. Noticing them consistently is reassuring. They are included in our consideration, which is an experience most parts have never had. Using parts language invites them and us to see the whole panorama of parts and their interplay. To go from feeling invisible to being heard and taken seriously is reparative.

## Differentiating Past from Present

For trauma treatment to be effective, no matter what methods we employ, we must be able to distinguish past and present—that is, to differentiate being threatened from being triggered. Without this ability, we will assume that what *feels* threatening *is* dangerous. As you probably have experienced, it is not difficult to implicitly reexperience the past. When our parts' survival responses are triggered in daily life, we continue to feel unsafe, and the parts feel confirmed in their belief that they face immediate danger. It becomes challenging to be here now, especially when the body is communicating, "Danger, danger—red alert!"

We now know that, as important as it is to acknowledge the past, it is even more crucial for traumatized individuals to stay connected to the present time. Acknowledging the past or observing the past intruding into present experience is very validating: "Of course, I have parts that are sensitive to disappointment! After so many false promises, why wouldn't they be sensitive to disappointment?" The past does not have to be denied or avoided. It simply is.

Our first priority must always be to challenge this subjective perception that trauma symptoms are indicative of current danger—or, equally problematic, proof of our fault or defectiveness. We must also know that we are safe *now* to effectively integrate how unsafe it was *then*. But all of that can be challenging when we are flooded with the parts' defensive responses and feeling memories, and when we are not using the language of parts. To make that clear distinction between past and present, we need to use the Noticing Brain (i.e., notice the uncomfortable feeling), speak using the language of parts (i.e., name it as a part), and acknowledge that the part got triggered. Whenever you say, "The hopeless part got triggered" rather than "I feel hopeless," you are differentiating threats from triggers, past from present.

## The Process of Recognizing That We Are Blending with Our Parts

Remember that the moment a trigger precipitates feeling memories and survival responses, the prefrontal cortex shuts down, and we lose our ability to think. Without the capacity for mindful awareness, we become flooded with intense feelings and impulses, causing the mind and body to *blend* with the parts, and we become whatever they feel.

> *When Annie felt the triggered sensation of painful loneliness and said to herself, "I'm so lonely and alone," she would blend with her child parts' feeling memories of rejection and neglect. Their painful feelings would flood her body, tears would come to her eyes, her heart would hurt, and there was no overt sign that these emotions were not hers. Unaware that her protector parts kept her at a distance from other people, especially potential friends, she would interpret her isolation as a statement about her unlovability and inability to please. She had no way to know that her interpretation reflected what the parts believed: that how they were treated had to do with their shortcomings, not with the failure of adults who were supposed to care for them. When she "blended" with the parts' feelings and beliefs, it confirmed their worst fears: They were still failing to please other people and failing to win their love.*

Blending with the intense feelings and physical reactions of parts is automatic for most of us. We feel the emotions in our bodies and assume that is what we ourselves feel. We don't ask, "Whose feeling is this? Is it my feeling or the feeling of a part?" When we blurt out a feeling or lash out at a loved one, we might say, "That was a mistake," but we assume that it is *our* mistake, not the expression of a part.

Blending poses two problems: First, it intensifies the part's feeling or belief because we second what they feel. By blending with them, we confirm their shame or hopelessness or righteous anger. Second, blending can cause the feelings to dictate our choices and actions. For example, when a depressed part's hopelessness is consistently confirmed by our blending with it, the sense that there is no hope and no future intensifies. In response, we may give up trying or begin wishing we were dead. When a suicidal part's impulse to violently end our lives is confirmed by blending, we are at risk of acting on impulses to harm ourselves.

Learning to recognize blending takes practice. If blending is your automatic response, as it is for most of us, then the priority is to recognize it. If you are already noticing and naming distressing feelings as parts, you are on your way. If you are already using the language of parts, that will help too.

When we blend with our parts, we join our parts in their sense of alarm or shame or their feelings of worthlessness. Now, there is no one to see and hear them—or to offer them a different perspective. Our decisions are based on their impulses and beliefs, not on our Noticing Brain's observations. When a part says, "I'm worthless," we feel a sense of agreement and shame. When the ashamed part feels the burning intensity of the shame, the thought comes up, "I should be ashamed." In that blended moment, we might decide to hide under the covers or avoid the lunch date we made or even to self-harm to find relief. Whatever decision we make can easily trigger other parts with whom we're likely to also blend: A critical part might be judgmental and we think, "I'm furious with myself." Blending tends to lead to more blending, which leads to even more blending.

Here are some cues that will help you recognize when you are blended:

- The belief or emotion feels undeniably true.
- Your whole body feels the feelings or impulses.
- You can say the word *part* but not feel any separation from them.
- It's hard or impossible to be mindful, interested, or curious.

Recognizing when you're blended with a part takes practice, especially when these feelings and beliefs are so deeply familiar to you. Annie's story serves as a reminder of just how difficult it can be to catch yourself in these moments, but how, with practice, you can create some space between yourself (as the "whole you") and your parts.

*Although Annie was fluent in parts language, the painful loneliness she felt was so intense and so familiar that she invariably blended with it. The harsh accusations of a critical part, whom she had failed in life, were also so familiar that she never questioned it. It took months of practice in recognizing that she was blended before she could feel a little more space between the parts' feelings or beliefs and her Noticing Brain. At first, she practiced simply assuming that she was blended, even though the feelings still felt like her own emotions. Only as she became more skilled at unblending could she feel the relief experienced by her parts when she did unblend from them. When she could notice them as distressed parts and notice herself observing them, the parts felt seen and heard. That in itself was a small but important piece of healing. The neglected children inside were finally acknowledged after years of either being blended with or disowned entirely.*

All of these skills require that you use your Thinking Brain as well as your Noticing Brain. Take a look at **Worksheet 7, *Using Your Noticing Brain***. Although you need your Thinking Brain for many aspects of life, the Noticing Brain is the key to tolerating your emotions and relating to your parts. Use the worksheet to help you differentiate between the two brains.

## Practicing Unblending as the Key

Once you recognize that more intense states of distress are usually a sign of blending or that blending is the reason why you feel overwhelmed, try to follow these steps to start practicing unblending:

- Notice the distress, overwhelm, or critical thought. Turn on your Noticing Brain.
- Name it as a part: "The ashamed part is very upset."
- Notice and name the blending: "I'm really blended with that ashamed part."
- Remind yourself that blending with a part is abandoning it, letting it suffer.
- Bring your full attention to the part: Where is it hurting? What words is it saying? Have you heard those words or thoughts before?
- Use your hands to represent you and the part: Notice one hand as the part and name what you notice about it. Then use your other hand to represent the "whole you."
- Observe yourself noticing the part. Make sure that you remain present with the part, letting the gap between your hands represent the space between you. Now you can observe and feel the part, and the part can see and feel you there.

As unblending becomes a familiar skill, pause every time you notice a part and notice yourself observing it. If you start to blend again, go back to noticing the part and then trying to notice yourself. Sometimes, the hardest part is being able to notice and feel yourself there with the part. But the more you practice this skill, the easier it becomes to unblend, making it possible to pause and linger long enough to get to know the part a little bit. Try to be curious about it: What triggered it? Are its feelings familiar?

> **Worksheets 8a** and **8b**, ***Blending with Parts*** and ***Unblending***, will help you practice the skills of noticing when you are blended and then how to unblend. Make as many copies of either worksheet as needed. These are skills that take practice. Don't be surprised if you unblend from one part only to have another part pop up to let you know it's in distress too.

Remind yourself that the part is having feeling memories. You don't have to know exactly what it is remembering—you only have to remember that the feelings are understandable, that there was a reason why this part felt exposed or invisible or afraid of being killed. Acknowledging the enormity of what a part has experienced can also evoke a little bit of spontaneous compassion, as long as you are clearly asking, "What kinds of things has this part experienced?" rather than "What happened to me at this age?" Remembering the traumatic context can help you see this part as a helpless, innocent victim or a creative survivor. It will then be easier to see that this part did not deserve to be treated as they were.

*Suzanne struggled with suicidal feelings for decades before she was able to recognize them as a communication from a part. Her determination to die had frightened her husband and children and even her therapists for years. Only when she began to observe the suicidal determination as a part, and recognize when she was blended with it, could she see that a suicidal part had been trying to protect her by offering to end her life. When she wasn't blended, she could see it as a part with a mission. The suicidal part believed that her overwhelm and inability to tolerate stress or emotion would make all the parts vulnerable to perpetrators.*

*When Suzanne began to see the suicidal part was offering its help and she could unblend from it more consistently, she could thank it for such a generous offer. Once acknowledged and thanked, the suicidal part relaxed a little. Unblending from this part allowed it to be heard and validated. Feeling heard, it could relax its intensity enough that Suzanne had an increasingly easier time noticing it as a part rather than blending with it. And the suicidal part's crisis of confidence in her became a powerful motivator, spurring Suzanne to work even harder on tolerating her other intensely vulnerable parts.*

*As Suzanne worked to expand her tolerance for vulnerable emotions, the suicidal part became quieter. There was less need for its services. Although there are times it still advocates for ending her life today, she remains able to stay unblended. She now has a relationship with her suicidal part rather than becoming it.*

## Cultivating Empathy

As you learn to mindfully notice your child parts' distress and validate their pain, it gets a little easier to understand or empathize with them. Empathy is not always easy to achieve because distancing ourselves from the trauma requires that we disown, loathe, and despise our parts' feeling memories. Empathy is the opposite of self-alienation, the opposite of denial and disowning. It requires that we risk getting so close to the parts that we start to become flooded with their intense emotions again.

It is important to remember that our relationships with our parts are a complicated. Survival required dissociative compartmentalization. Learning to notice the parts, naming them using parts language, and unblending from them changes those relationships. These are very important processes that usually bring some measure of relief. While these steps are stabilizing and reparative, a more connected relationship is required if we eventually want our parts and ourselves to feel healed.

To slowly and safely cultivate empathy for parts, it is easiest to start by simply listening to them and responding kindly.

When you feel empathy for a vulnerable or protector part, you'll notice that both you and they feel that empathy in the body. If someone asked you, "Do you feel compassion for yourself?" you would most likely say, "Absolutely not!" But when you can say, "I feel bad for that part—I feel sad for her," notice that your body softens and relaxes a little bit. Parts can feel the empathy you extend to them, and it feels good within the body as a whole. Although human beings tend to put words to experiences of empathy ("I feel understood," "It feels like someone gets it, "I feel like you believe me"), attunement and compassion are actually felt through nonverbal experiences of warmth, relaxation, and a sense of connection—not just through words.

Because we each only have one shared body despite the presence of so many parts, any intervention that has a positive effect on our somatic experience will have a positive effect in some way on each part.

## Conclusion

There will inevitably be parts who want to tell all, or parts who tell and retell stories of the same events over and over again. Equally likely are parts who fight to keep the secrets of the past intact or who avoid going there because of the shame and vulnerability it will trigger. Because you may feel either or both at different times, it may help to remind yourself that the goal in trauma treatment is not to remember what happened. It's to be able to be *here* instead of *there*.

When we can be conscious and present in the here and now—and tolerate the ups and downs of normal life—we can heal the injuries carried by our parts: the injuries to innocence, to trust, to faith; the injuries to the body; and the injuries to the heart and soul.

Worksheet 7

# Using Your Noticing Brain

**The Thinking Brain** helps you remember facts, see cause and effect, and assess safety and danger. It can tell the story, but it can't change it.

**The Noticing Brain** is responsible for awareness of thoughts, emotions, and sensations. It observes with curiosity instead of judgment. It doesn't take sides.

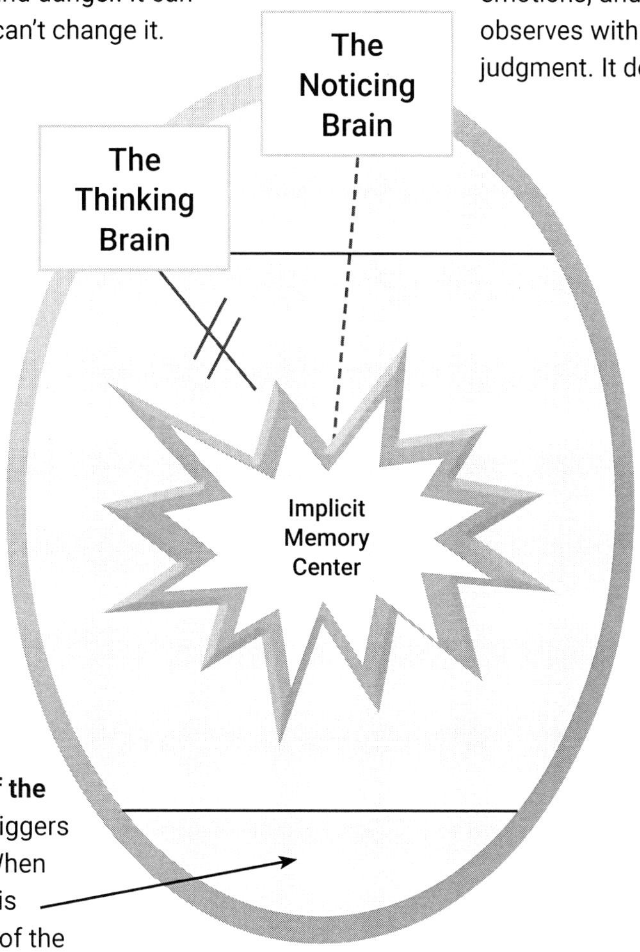


**The lower areas of the brain** respond to triggers by taking action. When the Noticing Brain is engaged, this part of the brain is calmer.

What do you know about these different brains of yours? Which do you rely on the most?

_______________________________________________

_______________________________________________

_______________________________________________

 

Worksheet 8a

# Blending with Parts

You can notice a part . . .

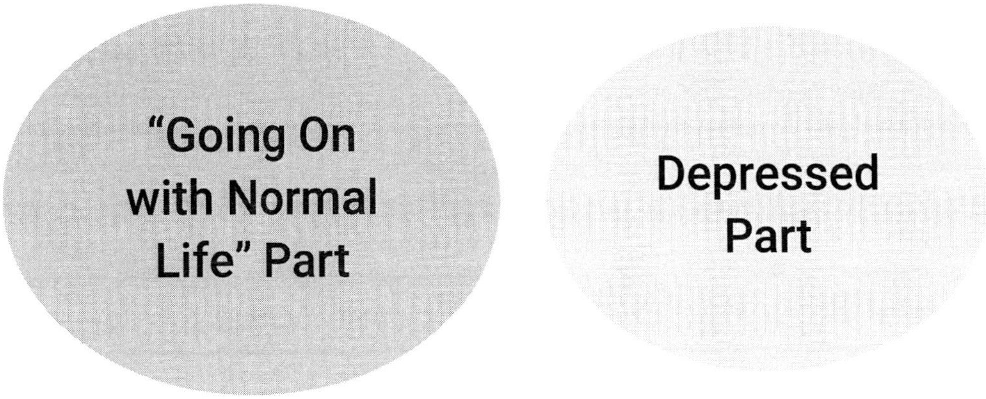


. . . or blend with that part . . .

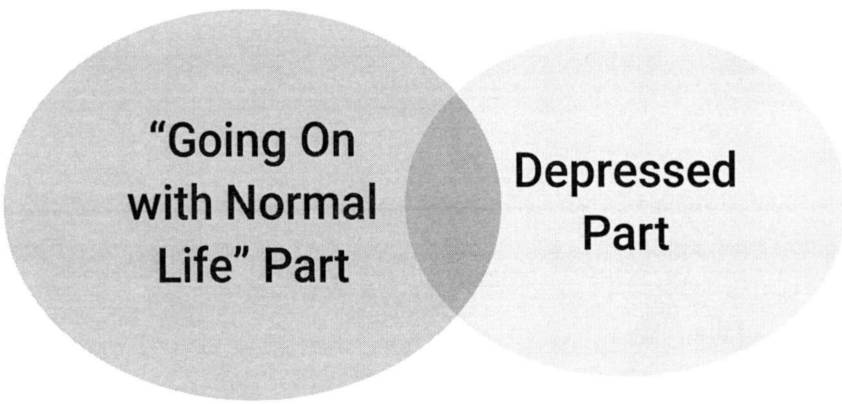


And then you feel depressed because you are flooded with its feelings and beliefs. What parts do you most often blend with?

___

___

___

Worksheet 8b

# Unblending

To unblend, you must first notice that you are blended:

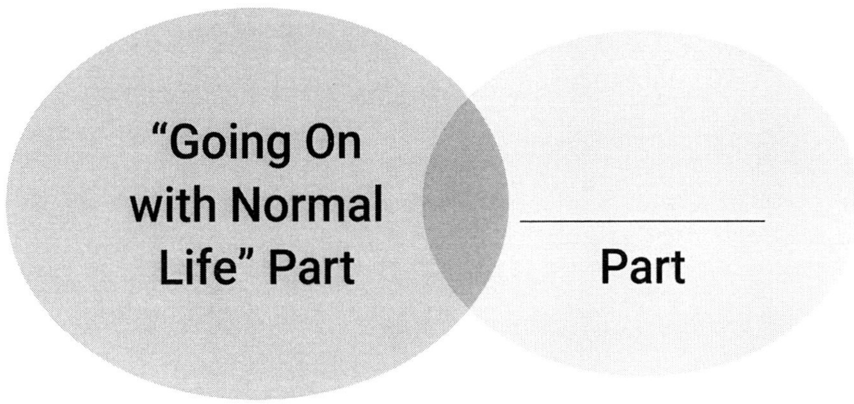


Once you identify that you are blended, the next step is to notice the feelings as the part's emotion: "The part is feeling ________________."

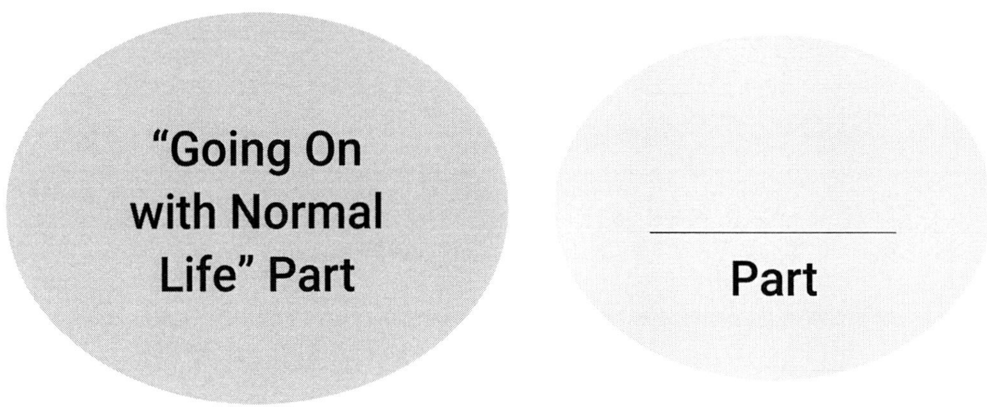


Use your Noticing Brain to notice the part *and* notice yourself as you observe the part. There are two of you here in this moment. Keep noticing the part's feeling as *its* feeling, and keep noticing you noticing the part. Notice both!

CHAPTER 5

# Befriending Our Parts and Learning to Communicate

It was once adaptive to avoid comfort or self-compassion. Relaxing one's guard is never safe in an unsafe world. Shaming or judging ourselves before others could do so was a necessary survival skill that helped us avoid being humiliated or punished. But when we want to recover from the effects of traumatizing experiences, those patterns hold us back. In order to heal ourselves and our fragmentated parts, we need to develop a relationship with them. And it must be a relationship to all of them: to wounded and needy parts, to parts hostile to vulnerability, to parts that survived through distancing and denial—to the parts we love, the parts we hate, and even the parts that intimidate us. When all parts of us feel internally connected and held lovingly in mind and body, they can begin to feel safe, protected, and nourished, often for the first time. That may seem like an impossible outcome to you right now, but you will get there in baby steps.

## Getting to Know Our Parts: The First Step Toward Relationship

So far, you have learned to identify distressing feelings as parts, notice their intense reactions, acknowledge the feelings as their *distress*, speak their language, and unblend from them so the parts can actually feel seen and heard.

The next step is to befriend the parts as you would befriend anyone, even a stranger, who has been through a painful experience. First, you must recognize them and their distress—you have to get to know them.

As you begin this process of getting to know your parts, it is important to first recognize how each part influences what you perceive and believe about the world. Before you can relate to them, you need to understand how they shape your experience.

Our observations of the environment, filtered through the telescopic lens of each part, often creates a distorted perspective. Each part has its own biases that narrow the aperture to what it expects to see while ignoring everything that falls outside that view. For example, the fight part is not scanning for safety cues; it is constantly hypervigilant for potential threats. The attach part, on the other hand, sees only the warm smile, the reassuring words, the things that make it feel special—while missing the danger signals that indicate grooming or seduction. The only threat it worries about is abandonment. The submit part doesn't notice the respect of colleagues or friends; rather, it is hypersensitive to any sign that confirms its beliefs of unworthiness or not belonging. When you learn to identify the lens through which you are looking—whether it's "Part of me is hoping to see someone who likes her" or "Somebody is looking at my husband's expression and thinking the worst"—and you pause to notice the part that's shaping that view, you can begin to get acquainted with it.

Mindfully noticing painful feelings as parts will help you tolerate emotions and sensations that may have previously felt intolerable, and it supports your ability to be curious, interested, and focused on what you are observing instead of trying to avoid or suppress it. Being interested is the first step toward getting to know another human being, even when that other is a part of yourself.

In the Internal Family Systems approach of Richard Schwartz (Schwartz & Sweezey, 2020), this observer role is ascribed to the *Self* with a capital S, an internal state that draws upon eight C qualities: curiosity, compassion, calm, clarity, creativity, courage, confidence, and connectedness. The Self is not just a meditative state, as each of these C qualities is an innate resource available to all human beings. We don't have to learn to be curious—we are born curious. Most importantly, access to these states creates an internal healing environment.

In TIST, there is also the fundamental assumption that these C qualities are accessible to any human being. They are never lost, no matter how sadistic and prolonged their traumatic experiences were. But accessing these qualities can be very challenging at first. It requires that the Noticing Brain be online, which alone often takes time and work. But even more complicated, feelings of compassion, calm, courage, and even curiosity can be triggering at times.

Start by noticing whatever part you can feel right now instead of reacting to or blending with it. Slow your mind enough so you can listen more attentively. As you *notice who is here*, be curious. Observe each thought or feeling as a separate communication: "A part of me is feeling overwhelmed and scared. Another part of me is judging her or maybe me. Does that part think I'm supposed to stop her from feeling scared?"

Try to be curious about both parts: Does it make sense that a part would feel small and scared? Does it make sense that a protector part would judge vulnerability as bad?

You might begin to notice a pattern: "I can see that the anxious part is interpreting the chaos in my apartment as something bad . . . Maybe because the critical part is having such a fit about it . . ." Does it make sense that there is a critical part trying to control your behavior or that of the wounded parts? How could it be trying to protect you?

"The hopeless part is really struggling today, isn't he? He doesn't want to feel this way—he doesn't want to be stuck in the past—but hopelessness and shame are his 'safe place,' and he's afraid that it's not safe to have hope." When you observe with curiosity, you begin to have a deeper understanding of the parts' reactions. You don't have to try to figure them out or make sense of them. Curiosity shows us the pattern and leads us to the questions we can ask.

Now that you've begun to notice how parts shape your perception, it's time to explore how they influence the stories you tell yourself—and how you can begin to relate to them with curiosity and compassion. Recognizing the difference between raw observation and the meaning-making process is key to understanding the deeper messages from your parts.

## Understanding the Stories Our Parts Tell

Trauma is an experience beyond words, and the interpretations we attach to a traumatic event or environment biases our meaning-making, leading to the creation of self-defeating stories. Which of your parts might write a self-defeating story?

The submit part is likely to write a shame-based, hopeless story explained by its defectiveness. "It's my fault" is its motto. The attach part is likely to tell a story of abandonment, of never being loved, of longing for someone to hear it. The fight part is likely to say that it's better to die than to continue being used and abused, better to fight to the death than surrender. Only the Going On with Normal Life part has access to the wider perspective of the prefrontal cortex and thus the ability to make meaning out of these apparently paradoxical feelings, beliefs, and instinctual reactions. It takes a sophisticated brain to recognize that the belief that you're just "faking it" might actually be adaptive in a traumatic environment.

With growing awareness of how parts interpret the world and shape your internal narratives, you can move toward forming more personal relationships with them. Like any relationship, this starts with curiosity and familiarity—learning to recognize who is speaking within you.

Parts do not wear name tags, nor do personality systems come with road maps or instruction manuals. Every part of us shares the same body, the same brain, the same environment. When we have a feeling or thought, it could be the expression of any part. To know *whose* feeling or thought it is requires familiarity: a personal relationship with the part that allows us to immediately recognize it when we hear its voice. It requires that we pause, listen carefully, and piece together the data or clues: Which part would have reacted to that trigger? What part would still feel ashamed right now?

When you become more deeply curious about a part, you can spontaneously begin to feel compassion toward it—in spite of yourself or in spite of other parts who are hostile to it. You might feel awed by the part's determination, touched by how little it is, amazed at its creativity in outwitting its captors, and astonished by how much pain it has endured while you were disconnected or dissociated from it.

Turn to **Worksheet 9**, ***Befriending Parts***, and practice using your Noticing Brain to relate to the parts you recognize. Observe how using the Noticing Brain makes it easier to spontaneously validate the parts you notice and recognize.

## Building Trust: Empathy, Mindfulness, and Presence

Simply observing and naming a part as a *part* is challenging enough, but the goal of healing requires even more. As our relationships with parts begin to take shape, we can go beyond naming and begin to feel for them. When empathy enters the picture, the connection becomes more than observational—it becomes heartfelt.

As you hear the parts' voices, sense their feelings, and name their appearance, add a tone of warmth or appreciation to your thinking. Describe their plight: "What was a little boy supposed to do?" Try to appreciate their contributions to your survival: "Had this part not given up and given in, what would have happened to me?" Try to see them as much more than disembodied implicit memories without a context. Think of them as inner people.

Admire the ingenuity of the very young part who tried to please his teachers: "That little boy was one smart cookie, wasn't he?" Or the courage of an adolescent part: "That 15-year-old was a determined young lady, huh? It was pretty amazing how she managed to get out of that home." If you are noticing self-destructive parts, try to see the *method to their madness.* What were they trying to achieve? The anorexic part's actions led to residential treatment, which was smart given the circumstances. The suicidal part signaled that something was very wrong, and someone else heard it. The 15-year-old alcoholic part found that beer took the edge off the pain and made it possible to sleep.

When you are so blended with parts' feelings and beliefs that you cannot mindfully observe them, you need other ways of stimulating the Noticing Brain. In those moments, creative tools like visual representation can help you stay in connection while gently unblending. Sometimes, it helps to use objects to represent parts. It can be as simple as using your phone to represent the part while you look at it. Imagine the phone as a part who is feeling the sense of failure you feel, and you are *you*, just observing that part. Does that help you to unblend? To see the part more clearly?

You can also use small toys, animal figures, or puppets to see a part more easily. Notice that each of these objects would be appealing to a child's mind, not just to an adult mind and body. Remember: Befriending your parts means communicating to little children as well as to guarded teenagers and hypervigilant adults.

Objects can help reveal patterns as well: "Notice how it all began when Sam was late, which triggered my little part—she felt so hurt, disappointed, and unimportant to him. Then the hopeless part got triggered, which triggered the fight part—and then I began to think about cutting myself!" Observe how suicidal, addictive, acting-out, or self-destructive parts get triggered by vulnerable parts' emotions and then emerge to offer those parts a way out of their distress. Moments of clarity like this confirm that the underlying purpose of self-destructive parts is to bring relief and regulation to the body: the very opposite of trying to die.

These practices help us remain present even when it's difficult. Staying with our parts, especially when they are in pain, reinforces that we are here now—willing to listen, to feel, and to stay. This is how trust is built.

Most people spontaneously respond to painful or distressing feelings by trying to ignore or suppress these feelings. Who wants to feel distress? But when we have parts, ignoring their feelings simply recreates the neglect of the past. Abusive caretakers are rarely aware of a child's feelings, or they exploit them as a reason to punish the child. The same is true of abusive partners or homophobic or racist neighbors. Now, years or decades later, the parts feel equally ignored and unimportant. If you are someone who suppresses your feelings, your parts might feel deliberately rejected, told to shut up. Maybe they have gotten the message, "I'm not interested in how you feel." These patterns will not foster healing.

Your job in the recovery process is to stay focused on the part and maintain an empathic state of mind, hard as that might be: "She's telling me how humiliating it was when other kids made fun of her." If you were to hear the story of any abused child who was laughed at by her peers, you would feel for that child. Try it with your part: Can you stay with whatever part you are sensing inside you and feel for that part? Or, if you can't feel empathy, work on just feeling kindly toward a part who was hurt in that way.

As you build trust through your presence and compassionate observation, the next step is to establish two-way communication. Listening to your parts is how you begin to develop a relational dialogue—not just noticing them, but truly hearing what they want to communicate.

## Learning to Listen: Dialoguing with Our Parts

Sharing the same body and mind is an advantage when it comes to internal communication. You feel what the parts feel, and they feel what you feel. But as is true in abusive or neglectful families, there is no back-and-forth verbal conversation about all these feelings. All the communication is nonverbal.

Learning to communicate with your parts is easier than you might think. One of the simplest and most powerful ways to start is by just asking questions internally, with genuine curiosity and care.

Notice a part that's uncomfortable right now. Name what you're noticing so it knows it's being seen. Unblend if you are blended with this part. And then ask it: "What are you worried about?" "What just scared you?" or "What's making you so angry?" Or you can ask, "Who's having a hard time right now?" Most of the time, parts answer, and you will hear their responses as thoughts, or you might hear their voices. Sometimes, they respond with a feeling, like anxiety or emotional shutdown. Assume that, too, is a communication. The question "What are you worried about?" works for almost every part. Each has their own worries, and even the fight part will acknowledge its concerns when asked. "What are you worried about?" also communicates your concern for the part. You might want the suicidal part to stop plotting your demise or be tired of blending with it, but asking "What are you worried about if I live?" is a question that invites a dialogue.

Internal communication takes practice and builds trust. Use **Worksheet 10, *Internal Communication***, to practice having an internal dialogue with your parts. It will be easier to first practice this when your parts are not so distressed. That will make it easier to use this skill when your parts are more overwhelmed and overwhelming.

Usually, the worries your parts initially express tend to be superficial. They might express a fear of making a mistake, being hurt, or being judged or rejected. The next step is to inquire more deeply, just as you would with a person in distress: "What is he worried about if someone judges him?" "What is she worried about if she makes a mistake?" In the light of the traumatic past, would it make sense that this part has a fear of being judged? Why might this part be terrified of making a mistake? The purpose of this step is not to retrieve memory. Making just enough of a connection between the past and present increases your empathic understanding of the parts' emotions and cultivates attunement. "No wonder the ashamed part won't give up her shame—it kept her safe. It was a way to survive—it doesn't mean it's true, but it worked then."

To suddenly hear that we care about their worries or understand why they are so worried is a new experience for traumatized parts. Some feel touched, some feel enormous relief, and some will become wary and mistrustful. Whatever the part's reaction to your interest or understanding, try to validate it: "I understand why you don't trust someone offering you kindness . . . it wasn't ever safe" or "I understand—no one ever cared how you felt before." Suicidal parts are usually afraid that you are too vulnerable to be safe in the world, addict parts are afraid you can't handle the emotions of the younger and wounded parts without substances, and people-pleasing parts are afraid of rejection or abandonment. These are all legitimate worries for parts who live in the feeling memories of the traumatic past, and they need your validation as evidence that you have heard them.

To ensure that the parts feel the sense of someone listening and caring, it is essential to maintain an unblended felt connection to the part. How does the part respond to your empathy or indignation on its behalf? What is it like for the part to hear that someone is actually interested in how it feels?

Sometimes, we try to say all the right words to our parts without any embodied connection to our words or feelings. These parts, however, are very perceptive. They have learned the hard way that people don't always mean what they say. If they don't sense that you are really there with them, they will not trust your words.

*Annie kept repeating to her parts, "You're safe now—you don't have to be afraid anymore." But it had no impact on their fears or survival responses because she hadn't befriended them yet. For them, it was like a stranger walking up and telling them, "You're safe." Some parts may have thought she was trying to trick them. It took many months of befriending them before any parts were willing to have a conversation with her about anything. For them, empty reassurances were a sign of being groomed, tricked, or exploited.*

*Annie would go on to discover that her parts first needed her to understand their fears and to remember that these fears had once been their daily reality. She learned to ask her parts, "What would you need to trust me a little bit more? What would tell you that?" These moments of genuine interest in how the parts felt were antidotes to traumatic abuse and abandonment.*

As you grow more confident in dialoguing with your parts, the next challenge is relational—how do you treat the parts that frighten you, frustrate you, or overwhelm your life? This section invites you to take on a new role: that of a wise host and internal leader.

## Welcoming and Leading: Creating Internal Community

Many people might be tempted to ask, "Why should I become a warm and welcoming host to trauma-related parts when they are turning my life upside down?"

The first thing to remember is that parts do not complicate our lives on purpose. There is no way to prevent triggers and triggering. The parts didn't ask to be dissociated and disowned. Our brains did that for us before we were old enough to have a plan for survival.

Second, we owe a huge debt of thanks to our parts. Never forget that they enabled us to survive intact! They allowed us to build a life after trauma. We owe it to our parts to welcome them like returning soldiers and to provide a healing environment for them.

In TIST, there is no emphasis on discovering what happened in the past. The focus is on the relationship between us and our parts now, on what is happening in the present moment. There is an implicit assumption that these parts are driven by the experiences of the past, by painful body and emotional memories. We can acknowledge that, but we don't make any effort to connect the parts' reactions to specific events. The parts may connect us to particular times and places, but they do so because they want to be understood and protected, not because they want us to know what happened.

To step into the role of a wise host, don't be afraid to ask yourself, "'Who is speaking right now? What is this part trying to tell me?" Then try to make decisions that consider the well-being of the *whole*. A diligent, hardworking submit part might try to get you to stay late at work, triggering the fight part's sense of being exploited and the attach part's fear that no one cares. When your Noticing Brain can see their conflicts, you will then see the potential solution that is right for *everyone*.

However, the intensity of our parts' trauma responses often drowns out a felt connection to our Going On with Normal Life selves, as much as we try to keep on going despite all the triggering. It is not surprising that our dogged persistence in trying to create a normal life is often perceived as *pretending* or *fraudulent*. It is counterintuitive to think of an authentic part that thinks and acts rationally and functionally despite the overwhelming sensations and emotions. It takes an understanding of trauma to see that dissociation allows us to live two parallel lives: one life in the nuts and bolts of daily living, and one life in the living legacy of the traumatic past. It is important to remember that dissociation is a mental ability often stimulated by traumatic situations. It is normal to live two parallel lives when that was required for survival. This system of parts tells us the story of how we survived the past, while the way we live each day tells the story of how we've grown thanks to our innate drive to continue.

Therefore, rather than thinking of the Going On with Normal Life part as an empty mechanical "chief of functioning," it is important to see that how you have carried on reflects something about yourself. Who you are as a grown adult is the person you became in spite of the trauma.

Your *parts* represent what you've been through, while *you* represent what you have made of your life despite the trauma. If you are a hard worker, caring friend, animal lover, artist, or intellectual, that says something about who you are as a person. The choices you've made or the direction you've taken reflect your values, your passions, or sometimes necessary adaptations to your circumstances. You may have had to work to pay the rent, care for children, or navigate challenging relationships, but *how* you met those challenges is a reflection of who you are. Of course, the choices each of us has made can be complicated by parts too.

*As a young adult, Annie was always drawn to children, and children were always drawn to her. She had an intuitive gift for engaging them in play and learning. But some of her protector parts believed that she could only be safe if she were a person of importance who was recognized for her achievements. Another group of protectors opposed the achievement parts, believing that it wasn't safe to leave her property. They repeatedly sabotaged Annie's efforts to play a more visible role in her community. They allowed her to get an online master's degree in teaching, but they wouldn't let her hold a teaching job outside of the home. Instead, they allowed her to informally help children in crisis by offering them a safe place and support to turn their lives around. Ten of those children are now functioning adults living stable positive lives. She was allowed to foster rescue animals, paint her house, trim hedges, and mow the lawn. But none of that pleased the parts who wanted public accomplishments. Believing them, Annie felt like a failure in life.*

*It was only through the experience of unblending from and befriending her parts that Annie began to have any connection to who she was. When she could finally see the world she had built for herself through her Noticing Brain instead of through her parts, she began to have a better sense of who she had become. She lived in an old farmhouse in the country with a husband, two grown children, and an extended family of choice—all people who cared about her and considered her central to their lives. She had all the right life experiences to offer a home for her traumatized child parts just as she had for all those surrogate children she had helped.*

The Going On with Normal Life part is the part of each of us that keeps on trying even when all the other parts are in turmoil and even when life gets hard. It takes a lot of courage and determination to keep on keeping on when your parts are freaking out. When you feel fraudulent, remember that a false self wouldn't be working this hard! Rather than doubting yourself for functioning, appreciate the strength it takes to go on with life even when you are overwhelmed and blended. Your *keeping on keeping on* provides a stable environment for your parts, even if it's less stable than you would like. Stability communicates that you will keep your parts safe.

Your internal leadership grows just by living your life in the present and staying in relationship with your parts—not through conflict, but through compassionate alliance.

## Living in Harmony: Acceptance and Mutual Support

Once you begin to feel curiosity and even compassion for your parts, the next step is to imagine how you might offer them a helping hand. When you are not blended with them and are getting acquainted with them, it can seem easier to extend them a little more support.

This support becomes more sustainable when it's rooted in relationship with your parts. Self-acceptance and self-compassion are challenging for trauma survivors, but if you are accepting and compassionate with others, you can begin to extend that to your parts as well. Healing does not require perfection—it's about befriending instead of rejecting yourself.

When you pause to befriend your parts—to be curious and interested rather than dismissing or judgmental—you slow time. You no longer feel the urgency to do or be anything different. With your body in a calmer state, you can be more at peace, and, as a result, your parts feel more at peace. Self-alienation does not contribute to a sense of peace or well-being, even when it is absolutely necessary to survive. Self-alienation creates tension, pits parts against each other, communicates a hostile environment, and diminishes the self-esteem of every part.

Befriending your parts means that you radically accept that you share your body and life with them. Living in harmony with yourself requires living amicably and collaboratively with all of your parts, not just the ones with whom you feel comfortable.

## Conclusion

This chapter has guided you through a progressive journey—from learning to observe your parts with mindful curiosity to developing trust, engaging in dialogue, and ultimately becoming an internal leader who can offer support and acceptance. Along the way, you've been invited to recognize the perspectives of your parts, appreciate their protective intentions, and begin cultivating genuine compassion for even the most frightening or self-critical voices within.

As you continue this work, remember that the goal isn't to eliminate parts or force them to change, but to build a safe and respectful internal environment. Each act of presence, empathy, or curiosity helps your system heal from traumatic experiences and move toward a more unified and peaceful internal world. *Healing is not a destination—it is a relationship with all of who you are.*

Welcome your parts home, not as enemies to be subdued, but as survivors to be cherished. This is how you move from merely surviving to truly living.

Worksheet 9

# Befriending Parts

**You**

Use your Noticing Brain to relate to the parts you observe in distress.

| Anxious Part | Depressed Part | Protector Part |
| --- | --- | --- |
| Let the anxious part know you hear it. | Let the depressed part know you understand its hopelessness. | Acknowledge how the protector is trying to help you. |
| ______________________ | ______________________ | ______________________ |
| ______________________ | ______________________ | ______________________ |
| ______________________ | ______________________ | ______________________ |
| ______________________ | ______________________ | ______________________ |
| ______________________ | ______________________ | ______________________ |
| ______________________ | ______________________ | ______________________ |
| ______________________ | ______________________ | ______________________ |
| ______________________ | ______________________ | ______________________ |

What happens when you notice and validate these parts? Do you notice a difference in you? Or a difference in how each one responds to you?

________________________________________________________________________

________________________________________________________________________

________________________________________________________________________

________________________________________________________________________

Worksheet 10

# Internal Communication

To build any relationship requires communication, a two-way dialogue, that allows both parties to learn more about each other on a deeper level.

**"Going On with Normal Life" Part**

**Depressed Part**

Ask inside, "What would you say to this part to let it know you hear it?"

______________________________

______________________________

______________________________

**"Going On with Normal Life" Part**

**Angry Part**

What would you say to this part?

______________________________

______________________________

______________________________

“Going On with Normal Life” Part

__________________ Part

Ask inside, “What would you say to this part to let it know you hear it?”

____________________________

____________________________

____________________________

“Going On with Normal Life” Part

__________________ Part

What would you say to this part?

____________________________

____________________________

____________________________

Remember that internal communication is built with interest, curiosity, and compassion. Be curious about what these parts are worried about. Keep in mind that they are not used to being heard, so your interest will mean a lot to them.

 

# SECTION 3

# DEEPENING:

## Increasing Compassion by Understanding Attachment Trauma's Complex Impact

CHAPTER 6

# Attachment Trauma: When Love and Safety Collide

As we move into this next phase, we shift our focus to a deeper exploration of trauma's living legacy, particularly how early attachment wounds shape the internal world of our parts. In this phase, we begin to understand that the deepest conflicts we carry often arise not from what happened to us, but from *who* hurt us—especially when those people were the very ones we loved. Here, we'll explore how trauma and attachment intersect, giving rise to complex relational patterns, internal conflicts, and painful survival strategies that endure long after the danger is gone.

In previous chapters, we saw how each part of us developed with the urgent purpose of helping us survive. Some fought, others fled, and some froze, submitted, or clung for care. These parts, each heroic in their own way, carry implicit memories of danger. But when the source of that danger was also the person we loved most, a deeper fracture occurs—one that plays out in our relationships, our longings, and our defenses for decades to come. In this chapter, we explore how attachment trauma creates inner conflict and how we relive those dynamics every time we seek closeness.

## The Body Remembers Attachment

To understand how attachment trauma endures, we must first recognize that attachment begins not as a story we tell, but as a body we inhabit. Our early experiences of attachment are body experiences: being held, rocked, fed, stroked, and seen with warm, loving eyes. Babies take in the warm gaze, smiles, and gentle movements of their caregivers, and respond with smiles, vocalizations, and chuckles of delight. But children can also easily sense discomfort, whether it's the tension in a caregiver's body, a still or expressionless face, an irritable tone of voice, or rough movements. These early experiences, good and bad, are remembered not in words but in the form of body and emotional memories.

We are born with immature nervous systems that are often overwhelmed by loud voices, sudden movements, anxiety, or tension, as well as by all our other immature systems, including our sensory systems, gastrointestinal system, and even breathing and heart rate. In order for a child's nervous system to tolerate the highs and lows outside the womb, it requires a caregiver who soothes, comforts, distracts, cuddles, or plays to regulate the baby's mood when they are in distress.

Our attachment habits in later life reflect the closeness or distance that created the most safety for us in our original family environment. Some of us may automatically tense up in response to closeness or human touch. Some of us might melt into a hug from anyone or only from someone we know and trust. Some people develop the habit of avoiding even those closest to them or allowing themselves to feel close only to familiar people. Are you more comfortable alone or in the presence of others? Are you more comfortable just having someone there? Or do you need physical and emotional contact to feel comfortable?

## The Attachment Paradox: Longing and Fear

But what happens when the very person who feeds and rocks us also frightens or rejects us? This is where attachment trauma takes root—not only in the body, but in relational fears and confusion that persist into adulthood.

Because children's innate attachment behavior is organized around seeking closeness, parents who are neglectful and abusive pose a double threat. Not only does their threatening behavior evoke fear, but it also intensifies a child's yearning for closeness and protection. The very people we automatically seek out for comfort and safety become sources of danger when they are frightening instead of protective. In an unsafe world, our two most powerful innate drives (to attach and to defend) remain highly activated, often both at the same time.

The result is a child who is caught between two equally strong pulls: the yearning for closeness and the instinct to fight, flee, freeze, or submit. Too much closeness feels dangerous, but so does too much distance.

When both safety and danger come from the same source, children don't just endure—they adapt. But the adaptations available to them are limited by age and powerlessness. In many cases, the child attempts to gain control of the caregiving relationship in the only ways they can: by reversing roles, becoming overly helpful, or angrily rejecting the caregiver. These survival strategies—while ingenious—come at a cost.

In a world where the source of safety is also the source of danger, there are few ways that a young child can exert control over their situation. Research tells us that the most common way very young children try to exercise control is by soothing, reassuring, and helping their mothers and fathers (Liotti, 2011). Called *parentification*, the child becomes the caretaker of the parent. The other strategy is to fight by pushing the parent away, attacking them physically, and humiliating and devaluing them. It is a risky strategy in a world where parents are abusive and much more powerful. Researchers note this latter style is more common in boys, especially in response to parents who are hostile, whereas the caretaker style is more common in girls (Liotti, 2011).

The lived experience of traumatic attachment creates an unavoidable and painful paradox: Closeness cannot be trusted, but distance or aloneness is not safe either. Most abused children find that being alone and without protection creates greater vulnerability, but being in proximity is also not safe. Because we could not depend upon the protection of our caretakers, we become loath to rely on others, or we swing to the opposite extreme, believing that our only safety lies in pleasing them.

> Using your Noticing Brain to identify patterns related to unsafe attachment will help you be curious and interested rather than automatically blending with a part. Use **Worksheet 11, *Recognizing Traumatic Attachment*,** to anticipate these relational issues.

## Living the Legacy: Internal Conflict in Adult Relationships

As adults, these unresolved internal dynamics don't disappear—they surface in our most intimate relationships, often in ways that feel baffling or overwhelming to ourselves and our partners. While the attach part continues to yearn for care, the fight part believes that vulnerability is threatening, leading to a conflict between parts that reinforces old wounds instead of healing them.

### *The Attach Part's Yearning for Care*

When we have experienced attachment trauma, we develop an attach part that idealizes others, feels deeply hurt when there are no overt signs of caring, and suffers from chronic fears of abandonment. The bias of this part is that it believes the only safety lies in closeness, in being cared for, in not being separated. When this part experiences closeness, it is both a relief and a trigger. Its fears of abandonment typically intensify in relationships, often leading to increasing demands on the time and energy of friends or partners. The feeling memories of yearning to be special, comforted, or cared for trigger a hunger for contact that can become overwhelmingly intense. Because these feeling memories and the fear of abandonment are intensified—rather than soothed—by proximity, relationships often become complex and turbulent. When this part gets triggered, what began as the pursuit of a romantic partner becomes what feels like a traumatic environment.

As the attach part becomes more active and vulnerable in relationships, so do the fight and flight parts. The flight part might threaten to leave, while the fight part attacks the other person, accusing them of cheating, lying, or abandoning us. It can be very confusing and very triggering for partners as different parts react to them. When our partners then overreact or underreact to the parts' communications, a cycle of triggering can begin that is very destructive to the healthy relationship the two loving adults envisioned.

The attach part needs to feel that others are warm, connected, and attuned to its needs for care, as it never had the opportunity to internalize a sense of secure attachment. The flight part needs space and to be accepted for its need to come and go or keep distance. The fight part requires proof that others will not betray us and will meet the needs of the attach part. "Proof" sometimes means that our friends or partners will be subjected to tests of patience, challenging boundaries, and tests of loyalty. Meanwhile, the submit part just wants to please by complying with whatever the other person seems to want, increasing the fight part's mistrust and need for control.

Some of us might have submit parts that are more burdened and submissive, while others of us may have parts that are more compliant and pleasing. Your submit part might even strive to be the best friend or partner that the other person has ever known, trying to elicit positive feedback that the attach part desperately craves. However, the submit part's willingness to do whatever others ask does not lead to greater closeness because its submissive behavior triggers the fight part to perceive our loved ones as exploitive and controlling.

A key indicator that you are blended with a part holding attachment trauma is the degree of rigidity associated with your reaction to a friend or partner: Parts see the world as black or white, have difficulty processing new information, and can't widen their perspective to take in multiple points of view.

Each trauma-related part, driven by its particular defensive response, tends to be biased in its perspective on attachment versus safety. As parts are triggered on different days by different aspects of life, our partners, friends, or family are often understandably confused by the relational dynamics of the fight and attach parts. Beneath the militant counterdependence of the fight part, there is always an attach part whose longing and hurt are being defended, who is being protected by the avoidance of dependence. The attach part's implicit memories and unmet yearning for connection have been stimulated, and both feel emotionally unbearable. The fight part's distrust of connection has been equally heightened. The role of the trauma and the traumatized parts are likely to go unrecognized and untreated. Our worst fears seem to be coming true: Things are getting worse, not better.

## *The Fight Part's Vigilance*

Fight parts are generally the most hypervigilant and wary of attachment, and the least likely to trust others or their motives, especially when the relationship triggers the attach part's dependency and longing to be special. To the fight part, vulnerability isn't just uncomfortable—it's dangerous. It remembers what happened when we were small, dependent, and exposed to harm. And it has vowed to never let that happen again.

You might be able to recall indicators of an active fight part in your own relationship history: friendships that were dropped after recurrent conflicts, difficulties at work due to interpersonal struggles with bosses or colleagues, frequent breakups in relationships, the tendency to always pick the "wrong" person, or the need to always give more than you receive. Those can be signs that your parts have been triggered in relationships.

*Empathic failure* generally describes words or actions that disappoint or hurt our feelings—or, more accurately, the feelings of the attach part. Most of the time, these moments of empathic failure occur because a friend or partner is perceiving us as a competent, non-fragmented adult, not realizing that we are blended with a needy, lonely, and sad child part. While these words or actions might seem harmless when directed toward an adult, they are deeply hurtful when spoken to a child part with urgent hopes for care.

*Laura fell in love with her husband's caring, sensitive nature and his lack of defensiveness when her fight part criticized him. Neither of them were prepared for what would happen when he became a medical resident and could no longer be with her at home on a consistent schedule. Suddenly, he would be called to work in the middle of dinner, or after they had gone to sleep, or when he was supposed to put the children to bed. Laura panicked every time he was called. Blended with her attach part, she felt unbearably abandoned and afraid to be alone. She would beg and plead with him not to leave for the hospital, or she would run after his truck as he drove away. As soon as he returned from an emergency, he would be greeted by her fight part, enraged that he left instead of turning back. Their marriage was suddenly in shambles. Neither understood why Laura couldn't tolerate his having to respond to medical calls as all young doctors do. Rationally, she could understand that he didn't have a choice, but her parts could not.*

As in Laura's case, the attach part's panic and hurt triggered fight parts to vehemently defend themselves by attacking the person who caused them hurt: her husband. Unable to *see* Laura's little part in her grown-up body, he felt defensive, disrespected by an angry, demanding wife. Even when partners understand that their mates have experienced traumatic attachment and they feel remorse for having been hurtful, they also understandably feel defensive when they are criticized or found lacking in some way. Without the realization that an empathic failure represents the inadvertent wounding of a child part—coupled with the defensive efforts of an angry part seeking restitution—the partner's efforts at reparation may be misattuned. Simply saying, "I'm sorry I had to leave—I'm sorry I hurt your feelings" is not enough to soothe a wounded child part.

Vulnerability is the enemy of the fight part. At age one, three, six, or even ten, there is little a fight part can do to defend against abusive adults. Thereafter, any situation that evokes dependency or vulnerability is likely to activate the fight part. Hypervigilant and narrowly focused on threat, the fight part is biased by the traumatic reality that the people who are supposed to love you can reject, abuse, or abandon you. They can lie, manipulate, and misuse their power to control you. That is what the fight part has learned to expect.

Because the fight part has concluded that our vulnerability is open to being exploited by abusive adults, any relationship that evokes vulnerability is likely to be highly threatening. Unfortunately, most of us are at our most vulnerable in very close partner, family, or friend relationships.

> Becoming aware of the internal conflicts stimulated by relationships can help you work with parts rather than blend with them. Use **Worksheets 12a** and **12b**, ***Struggles in Relationship*** and ***Mindfully Noticing Internal Struggles***, to increase your ability to work with parts triggered by attachment.

## The Parts in Relationship

Understanding how these patterns play out is only part of the journey. Healing begins not only in our relationships with others, but in the way we learn to relate to the parts within us: those that still carry fear, yearning, anger, or shame. True transformation requires befriending the parts and learning to speak on their behalf.

Befriending our parts includes not just listening to how they feel. It also includes listening for their chorus of voices and the themes they communicate in relationships. Expecting that these parts will be triggered by friends and partners also helps, but that can be hard to do in the early stages of relationships when everything is going smoothly and easily. As the relationship becomes closer and more committed, or we become more dependent on the connection, the parts begin to be triggered more frequently.

Be ready for your parts to voice their positive feelings about your partner, and be ready for them to have negative reactions too. Using your Noticing Brain, name the themes and the parts as you hear them. Try to be as curious as you can about what triggered them and what they are communicating to you. They will need help from you to manage their hurt, desperation, anger, and unbearable feelings. Relationships are a big trigger when you have suffered traumatic attachment. It is common to have difficulty sustaining access to your Noticing Brain, noticing your parts, and staying unblended. There may be times when it's impossible to feel empathy for their feelings, or even to be curious, because their intensity takes over so quickly.

But your relationship can potentially flourish if you can help yourself, your parts, and your partner when you notice traumatic attachment triggers.

Remember that the goal of treatment is to develop increasingly close and healing emotional bonds between you and your young parts: the ones that are still afraid, still angry, still grieving what they never received, still feeling deeply ashamed and alone. You also need to grow your bonds with both the vulnerable parts and the protector parts. Though protectors are rarely explicitly vulnerable, you cannot forget that their attachment needs were never met either.

## The Importance of Honoring Our Parts

To the degree that we observe, speak, and connect from a place of authentic respect, warmth, and admiration for all our parts, each one can be seen as a potential resource—not just a liability, but a real inner person worthy of compassion. We must enthusiastically acknowledge the survival contributions of our fight and flight parts. We must treat them like the war veterans they are. These parts fought hard for a worthy cause: our survival. We must honor their service. The more we unblend from fight parts triggered by our relationships, the easier it is to thank them for offering to help. That simple thank-you communicates to them that they have been heard, have been respected, and are not needed to defend.

The submit and freeze parts often benefit from being honored too. Although their service consisted of avoidance strategies (e.g., freezing in fear, becoming mute, serving others, pleasing and self-sacrificing, floating up to the ceiling), they were essential to our survival and adaptation too. Without them, we might have reacted in ways that threatened the abuser and evoked far worse punishment. In our adult relationships, the submit part may be afraid to rock the boat, may give so much that our friends and partners stop giving equally, may be so focused on pleasing that there is no room to wonder what would please us. The submit part is the part that is afraid to say no or can't set boundaries with others, usually enraging the fight part.

We may need to honor the attach part for finding support wherever possible: from grandparents, teachers, the mothers of friends, neighbors. Those relationships offered us hope, provided us with role models, and even gave us the experience that we could be loved. In return, the attach part needs our support, comfort, and reassurance when it's feeling hurt, abandoned, or alone.

> *When Laura realized that it was her little-girl part that panicked when her husband left the house, she felt sorry for her: "I've been making life hard for me and everyone else," she thought. Immediately, she felt the impulse to care for her little girl and to help her. "I keep telling her she's in my heart—she'll never be alone because she's right here with me."*

It's easy and almost automatic for most of us to blend with an attach part's intense emotional pain, but when we do, we abandon that part all over again. The panic it feels is the memory of being little, overwhelmed, and unprotected—and unloved. When you feel your attach part's terror of abandonment, remember that it needs you to stay with it. Your loved ones may have to come and go, or they may be hampered by their own early attachment experience, but your attach part needs to feel your comforting presence. There is no *alone* if you are there.

## Conclusion

Attachment trauma is not just a story from our past. It is a living legacy, woven into our emotions, relationships, and even our nervous systems. The very instincts that once helped us survive—yearning, pleasing, withdrawing, defending—can now sabotage our search for connection and safety. When closeness evokes panic and distance feels like abandonment, it does not mean we are broken; it means we are remembering. Each part of us, whether it fights, flees, submits, or clings, carries wisdom born of necessity. These parts deserve not our judgment, but our curiosity, compassion, and care.

The healing journey is not about silencing these parts but, instead, listening to them—honoring the pain they hold, the roles they played, and the needs they still carry. As we learn to unblend from their intensity, we also learn to speak on their behalf, offering the presence and protection they never had. In doing so, we slowly become the safe attachment figure they have always longed for. And from this place of inner relationship, we can begin to forge healthier, more attuned connections in the world outside.

Worksheet 11

# Recognizing Traumatic Attachment

Recognizing the signs of traumatic attachment can help you better understand your relationships. Is there a part of you that puts up with too much? Or a part unwilling to put up with anything? Do parts of you want closeness while other parts want distance? What parts are most triggered in your relationships?

**Put a check mark by the triggers of traumatic attachment that you recognize:**

- ☐ Not being listened to ____________________
- ☐ When my partners and friends "don't get it" ____________________
- ☐ Lack of connection with others ____________________
- ☐ Fear of being abandoned ____________________
- ☐ Fear of being cheated on ____________________
- ☐ Being touched ____________________
- ☐ Being alone or apart ____________________
- ☐ Being ignored ____________________
- ☐ Fears that I am not good enough ____________________
- ☐ Being criticized or shamed ____________________
- ☐ Being around someone who is withdrawn and not speaking ____________________
- ☐ Compliments and expressions of affection ____________________
- ☐ Not having any alone time ____________________
- ☐ Someone who monopolizes the conversation ____________________
- ☐ Being asked how I feel or what I want ____________________
- ☐ Getting my feelings hurt ____________________
- ☐ Being around someone who is angry or uses abusive language ____________________
- ☐ Someone who doesn't do as much for me as I do for them ____________________

Be curious about which parts are sensitive to these different triggers. Next to each trigger, write down what parts you think are most affected by it.

Worksheet 12a

# Struggles in Relationships

Be curious about the internal struggles inside you. What triggers those struggles? What parts struggle most with the others? Is there conflict between vulnerable parts and protector parts? Draw lines between parts to show their conflicts.

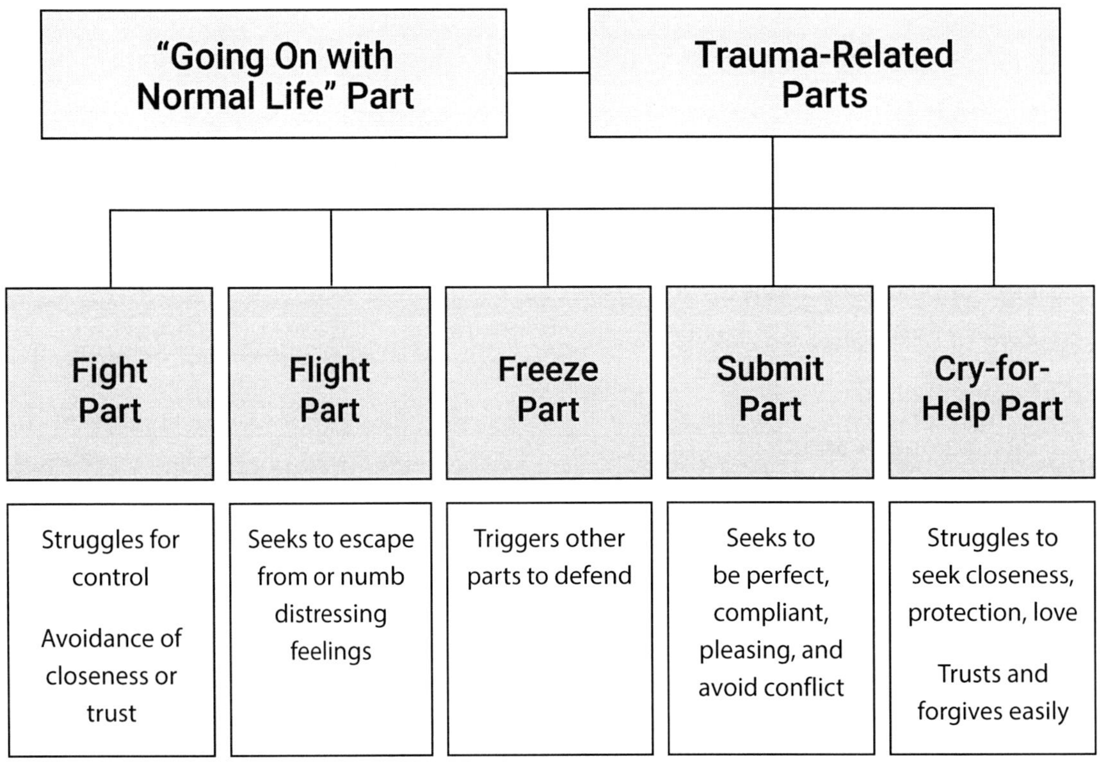


How do these conflicts affect your reactions?

________________________________________

________________________________________

________________________________________

Worksheet 12b

# Mindfully Noticing Internal Struggles

Practice using your Noticing Brain to just observe the internal struggles without getting caught up in them. They are not your struggles—they are conflicts between parts.

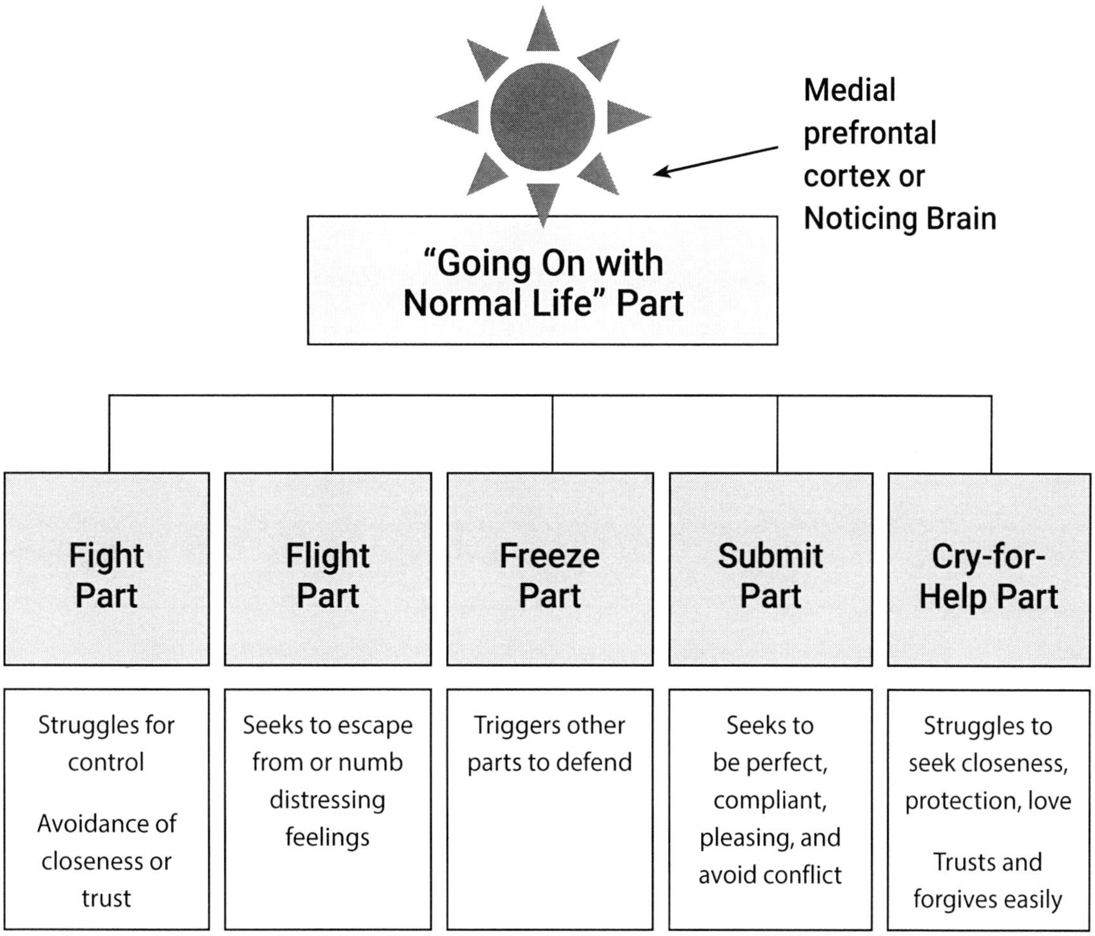


Which parts are most often in conflict with each other? Or with you? Which ones struggle the most? Which are most familiar to you? (Just notice, don't try to figure it out.)

______________________________________________________________________________

______________________________________________________________________________

______________________________________________________________________________

CHAPTER 7

# Understanding Unsafe Behaviors as Protector Parts

Surviving abuse, going on each day as if nothing has happened, and trying to navigate a traumatic environment would erode anyone's determination to live. Traumatized individuals live each day feeling helpless, overwhelmed, inadequate, terrified, and alone—there is nowhere to turn, nowhere to hide, no one to help. Because the bodily sensations and emotions connected to trauma triggers are still experienced as threatening by parts, this survival pattern remains instinctive. The alternating experience of having no protection from harm and the drive to survive in any way possible often remains a daily experience.

## The Legacy of Trauma: Desperate Measures in Desperate Times

Neglect or abuse quickly teach victims that it is safest to rely as much as they can on themselves. The feeling memory of that experience becomes a mission for protector parts like fight and flight. These parts instinctively seek relief through a variety of behaviors that share one common characteristic: None of them requires reliance on any other human being. When all seems lost, the fight and flight parts instinctively come to our rescue, offering to guard against dependency and find other ways out of vulnerability.

These protective efforts are often misunderstood, but they originate from an urgent need to create a sense of safety in an unsafe world. The fight part's offer to save the day by dying by suicide is often welcome. Having a sense that there is relief in sight, an exit plan, or a parachute brings a glimmer of hope to all the parts. The felt sense is "There is something I can do." If you have ever struggled with self-destructive impulses, ask yourself, "How old was I the first time I thought about dying as a way out?" Often, these thoughts come to us very early in life, long before we are physically capable of doing harm to our bodies.

Overwhelmed by what feel like dangerous feelings—and lacking a way to manage them—it's not unusual to experience our emotions as unbearable, intolerable, and life-threatening. Having learned to survive by dissociating or minimizing danger, dying is rarely what we fear. What feels dangerous is the feeling memory: "I can't tolerate these emotions by myself—if no one can help me, I will die."

## When Feelings Become Life-Threatening

The most common error made by professionals and survivors alike is the automatic assumption that self-harm, suicidality, eating disorders, and substance abuse are destruction-seeking, rather than relief-seeking, tendencies. If we assume that self-harm is meant to induce pain, then we interpret it as self-punishment. If we assume that suicidal thoughts reflect a conscious intention to die, we interpret them as a life threat. These assumptions miss the core issue: Self-destructive impulses reflect the pursuit of control over unbearable feelings driven by parts who are trying to protect us from harm.

The fact is that hurting the body, starving it, planning its annihilation, or compulsively engaging in addictive behavior all result in welcome relief from physical and emotional pain. The moments right after something bad has just happened are often the safest for victims in unsafe environments. Their parts learn from repeated experiences to seek actions that can lead to relief.

*Annie's protector parts had a pattern that she had accepted as normal for many years. Any physically demanding yard work, like raking leaves or shoveling snow, would trigger them to work harder and harder until she got injured or was in pain. Only then would they stop the strenuous effort, but Annie would suffer physically for days afterward, confirming her wounded parts' belief that people were still hurting them. It was only when she realized that this pattern was driven by parts seeking the relief of having survived pain that she could anticipate and work with them. She had to communicate her understanding that they wanted her to feel pain to be sure she was safe.*

As in Annie's case, protector parts are trying to solve a problem for us. The question is: How do we validate them without acting on their impulses?

To effectively treat unsafe and addictive behavior, we must address the central dilemma. If the parts that drive self-harming, disordered-eating, or addictive behavior do not trust us to manage vulnerable parts with distressing feelings, how do we gain their trust? If they are trying to protect us, how do we give them confidence that we don't need to be hurt or killed to save ourselves?

The first priority is to attend to their internal struggles: What triggers are activating them to such desperate measures? How are they trying to help? Most importantly, what are they so worried about?

## How Unsafe Behaviors Provide Relief

Child abuse and neglect, torture, domestic violence, and many other categories of trauma share a common characteristic: The victim's body, mind, and emotions have been exploited by others, whether to gratify their needs, exert control, or provide an outlet for the release of tension. Because the victim has been deprived of normal sources of tension relief (i.e., parental soothing), their body becomes no more than a vehicle for releasing tension, with no other real value. And if we believe that our bodies have no value, then it doesn't matter what we do to them.

The biggest challenge is how effective these methods are at producing relief. Before our bodies develop tolerance to these behaviors, any harm to the body (e.g., cutting, burning, hitting) has the same effect as any other injury. Initially, the physical injury stimulates adrenaline production, resulting in increased energy, focus, and feelings of control. This is followed by the release of endorphins (the body's "happy chemicals"), facilitating a relaxation effect and relief from pain. Both chemical releases act quickly, counteracting the distressing sensations and emotions.

In eating disorders, relief can be achieved by either undereating or overeating. In anorexia, restricted food intake results in numbed emotions and sensations, accompanied by an increase in physical energy. Overeating, on the other hand, results in numbness accompanied by relaxation, spaciness, or drowsiness. Bulimia also causes numbness due to both bingeing and purging. The problem is that as our bodies develop tolerance, we must restrict more severely, eat more, or binge and purge more frequently to find the same relief.

Substance abuse and addictive behaviors also result in quite specific effects—as reflected in the terms, *uppers* and *downers*. Uppers like cocaine, speed, MDMA, Ritalin, Adderall, crystal meth, and other stimulants are the drugs of choice when clients begin to feel dead or empty inside. But these uppers can also be used to increase feelings of power and control, or heightened readiness for action. (As you can imagine, fight parts often prefer the uppers.) Similarly, alcohol, marijuana, and benzodiazepines (downers) all soothe overwhelming emotions and help us maintain a chronic state of numbness. Opioids, such as heroin, oxycodone, and morphine, are downers that provide relief but also stimulate euphoria. Once addiction develops, any sense of connection between the drug and the trauma symptoms they once helped treat is lost. Also lost is the connection between the addiction and the protector parts who volunteered to take us out of our misery by starving, sedating, or hurting the distressed parts.

## Understanding Internal Conflict That Stimulate Protectors

If the desire for closeness is held by an attach part, the ability to appease by a submit part, the need for distance by a flight part, the fear of attack by a freeze part, and the drive to control by a fight part, then we have all the ingredients necessary to manage in a dangerous world. That each part can operate somewhat independently of the others creates an advantage. The parts scan the environment for signs of danger and react to each trigger in their own characteristic ways. Tragically, those who could support the healing process often trigger the parts, especially protector parts, just as much as people who are indifferent or want to harm us.

In the moment, self-destructive actions stem from a *perfect storm* of variables. First, a trigger evokes the parts' painful emotions and shuts down the prefrontal cortex, disempowering the Thinking and Noticing Brains. Then, the fight and flight parts have free rein to act on their survival instincts by taking some action intended to bring relief, whether it is bingeing and purging, cutting, attempting suicide, taking a substance, or restricting food. For a short time, there is a temporary feeling of relief. And because there is little felt connection between the apparently benign trigger, the hurt and sadness of wounded parts, and the impulsive behavior of the protector parts, the only way to understand the impulses is to interpret them as intentional: "I want to kill myself," "I can't let myself eat," "I need a fix." You may logically believe that you don't approve of hurting your body, using drugs, or bingeing or restricting, but the impulses of protector parts are very intense, and blending with them is hard to resist.

When self-destructive behavior is labeled as pathological, borderline, or manipulative, attention is diverted away from the underlying issue: the internal struggle between the parts. Parts whose bodies were hurt, deprived of food, or even drugged are frightened by the relentless self-injury and self-starvation of fight and flight parts. Successful treatment of any conflict requires acknowledging all parties involved, not just those on whose side we are. But when we have no hope for the future, feel deeply vulnerable, and experience strong impulses to take drastic action, it is hard to believe that simply *keeping on keeping on* will have much chance of success—unless we know that the hopelessness and vulnerability we feel belong to our traumatized parts, and the impulses to *do something* are driven by our protector parts. To resolve these internal struggles, we have to learn to see the parts and trust their positive intentions without acting on their impulses. They are all committed to survival in different ways. Even the most intensely suicidal parts "want to die in order to live."

## Staying Unblended and Differentiating Yourself from the Protector Parts

When you feel the wish to die, the questions you must always ask yourself before jumping to any conclusion or action are: Which part feels suicidal? The depressed part? A suicidal part? What triggered this part or parts?

Once you deconstruct the meaning behind the suicide threat, you uncover what's really underneath: "My depressed part just wants to go to sleep and never wake up again" or "My attach part is really sad and disappointed, and the fight part is trying to protect it by convincing me to end my life." Each of these answers requires a different solution, which you cannot provide without an understanding of the parts.

You must always differentiate the intentions of a part from its actions: What is the suicidal fight part hoping to accomplish? How is it trying to protect me? Where is my Thinking Brain? Why is it missing in action? Is my Noticing Brain also temporarily disempowered by the intense emotions and impulses of parts? Or is it just watching helplessly from a distance?

The biggest risk to our lives posed by suicidal or self-destructive parts results from blending with them. Keeping all the parts safe requires that we repeatedly and consistently translate distressing emotions into parts language, connect the unsafe impulses to protector parts, and differentiate their beliefs from our own so we can stay unblended. When we notice an impulse to cut or the urge to drink, it is important to name it as a part's impulse. Then, by noticing ourselves noticing the part, we can begin to put some space between ourselves and the part. We can notice what *we* believe about self-injury, drug use, or suicide versus what the protector part is advocating for.

Be curious about what this part is worried about or the problem it's trying to solve. As painful as our emotions sometimes are, they are the feelings of parts. Would you try to drug someone or starve them to make them stop crying? Would you hurt or threaten to kill them? Observe the arguments and impulses of the protector parts as ***their*** feelings. The goal is to have your Noticing Brain there with you, reminding you that "It's just the fight part—you don't have to do what it wants."

> Turn to **Worksheet 13** to notice the protector parts in you. Be curious about how each one is trying to help or protect. That will help you recognize them when they are triggered in your life.

## Anticipating Triggers of Parts

Suicidal and self-destructive protector parts are typically activated by the distress of younger parts. So, your major focus should be on recognizing and soothing these vulnerable parts before fight and flight parts feel like they must act.

Now that you have learned to recognize the signs of distressed parts, use your Noticing Brain to observe them and name their emotions as their own. Practice simply staying aware of them without blending. The same events or people in your life will trigger the same parts over and over again. Rather than always trying to recover from their being triggered, wouldn't it be more helpful to anticipate the next upcoming trigger?

Take note of domino effects, of patterns in which triggered parts trigger other parts who eventually trigger fight or flight. A typical domino effect might start with an attach part that gets triggered by being ignored, which stimulates a depressed and hopeless part that feels unlovable, which in turn triggers a fight or flight part.

Typically, depressed parts trigger the unsafe impulses of protector parts. Sometimes, young attach parts or parts who communicate via flashbacks and memories can also trigger them. Ashamed parts can also be triggering for protector parts, evoking a painful vulnerability that is intolerable to any part whose biological imperative is to gain control over the enemy.

## "No Part Left Behind"

Traditional treatment models emphasize abstinence from and rejection of unsafe behavior, but that can easily be interpreted by protector parts as a rejection of *them*. Why would we want to reject a part that is trying to help? It makes much more sense to unblend from a protector's impulses and to initiate a dialogue with it. Why would we want to kick that part out?

Our motto should always be: "No part left behind." We must never allow ourselves to abandon parts responsible for having helped us survive. The ashamed part, the frightened part, the addicted or eating-disordered part, and the suicidal, angry, self-injurious, or justice-seeking part all deserve our respect and compassion. When we hold ourselves to the "no part left behind" standard, we take the threat of abandonment off the table. That threat no longer hangs over their heads. This is a reparative experience for the parts: Someone has heard them, understands them, and has pledged not to abandon them in what they feel is a dangerous world.

In a world that feels safe (or safer) to our parts, we can collaborate to cocreate a life that is not dictated by trauma. Each part can play a valuable role after trauma too. Beyond carrying survival responses, our parts have important resources related to their specialized roles. For example, the fight response gives us increased energy, determination, a "backbone," and the ability to stand up for our rights and privileges. As you learn to ask the fight part to give you the courage to say no or to give you the strength to hold your ground, you will feel a surge of energy or increased strength in your body. Other parts feel safer when they feel that energy. The freeze part feels a physical sense of being protected; the submit part won't be taken advantage of as easily and will have energy to counteract its hopelessness; and the flight part doesn't have to run for cover because all the parts are safe *here now*. No part has to be left behind because all of them have something of value to contribute to our whole.

## Conclusion

Understanding self-destructive behaviors as protective strategies reframes the narrative of trauma from one of shame to one of ingenuity. Each impulse that once seemed chaotic or dangerous now reveals a part fighting to preserve life in the only way it knew how. These parts—no matter how extreme their actions—are not the enemy; they are loyal defenders of our most vulnerable selves.

To move toward healing, we must become compassionate leaders within, capable of witnessing pain without judgment, of honoring the past without reenacting or reliving it. Healing is not achieved by silencing or banishing our parts but by listening, learning, and offering them new roles in a life no longer ruled by danger.

When we see our protector parts not as problems to eliminate but as allies to understand, we transform our internal landscape. We are no longer fragmented survivors of past harm—we become integrated systems, with each part valued, each need acknowledged, and each voice heard. In this way, we move from surviving to truly living.

Worksheet 13

# Working with Your Protector Parts

Protector parts often do not feel protective. When their protection involves self-harm, substance abuse, suicidal feelings, or self-judgment, you may feel less unsafe, rather than more protected. Put a check mark by protector parts you recognize, then identify how they might be trying to help you.

| **Recognizing protector parts:** | **How are they trying to help?** |
|---|---|
| ☐ Inner critic parts | ______________________ |
| ☐ Suicidal parts | ______________________ |
| ☐ Self-harming parts | ______________________ |
| ☐ Eating disorder parts | ______________________ |
| ☐ Substance abusing parts | ______________________ |
| ☐ Angry parts | ______________________ |
| ☐ Violent parts | ______________________ |
| ☐ Shutdown parts that allow no feelings | ______________________ |
| ☐ Parts that isolate | ______________________ |
| ☐ Mistrustful, suspicious parts | ______________________ |

Assume these parts are present because they once helped you survive and adapt in an unsafe world. Understanding them as protectors will help you change your relationship with them and change their relationship with you.

SECTION 4

# REPAIRING:

## Offering Reparative Experiences to the Parts as the Path to Cultivating Internal Secure Attachment

CHAPTER 8

# Restoring What Was Lost: Creating Healing Relationships Through Safety, Connection, and Repair

The inner world tends to be a battleground. Protector parts, believing their present environment is as malevolent as the traumatic environment of the past, want none of it. Meanwhile, the attach part's yearning for closeness or unconditional trust instigates the fight part's determination to defend against any and all emotional connection. It is often an endless cycle. Flooded with the parts' emotions, impulses, and beliefs, our tendency is to assume that their triggered feelings represent our reality. There is little or no felt sense of having accomplished something in *keeping on keeping on* when we are still suffering the effects of traumatic experience.

*Despite her stable and normal home life, Annie found her day-to-day experience dominated by traumatized child parts, with unfortunate ramifications. Although she wished for more contact with others (and so did her attach part), her fight and flight parts held her back from acting on that wish. Instead, she was internally compelled to isolate, avoid going outside, and never, ever answer the door or telephone. Only those individuals seeking caretaking in her home were allowed to have contact with her. Ironically, caretaking had been the safest role in her family, and many parts did not want to give it up despite the scathing criticism of the judgmental part. Feeling a sense of defectiveness because of her symptoms and difficulties, Annie had no idea how much blending with her parts was impacting her life and sense of identity.*

## Blending, Avoidance, and Internal Alienation

It is extremely challenging to forge a relationship with our parts when we are blended with them and cannot connect to any other feelings or knowledge. The parts keep crying out to us for help, but we are overwhelmed by their screams. Most of us instinctively try to avoid or suppress our parts' feelings, often by trying to talk them out of their feelings: "You don't have to be afraid—you're safe now." But when we don't stop and listen to them, the parts feel abandoned, just as they did in their abusive environments. Our disconnected reassurance that they are safe now is often more alarming than reassuring. The parts' experience is that empty reassurances are usually a lie told by someone trying to exploit them.

*Although Annie went through the motions of relating to her parts, she had no emotional connection to the words she spoke to them. In fact, she was afraid to feel too much for her young selves, finding it overwhelming. Although she often blended with her parts, the idea of feeling empathy for them was appalling to her: "I'll drown in their feelings," she insisted.*

For many trauma survivors, the past—as conveyed by the incessantly triggered feeling memories of the parts—is experienced as more real than the present. When that happens, we and our parts continue to relive and relive, over and over, the neglect, rage, fear, and dread. Our wish to be free of their feelings leads us to recreate a traumatic environment in which we repeatedly abandon and ignore our parts just as they were abandoned in the past.

Blending is no better than avoiding the parts. It, too, confirms that they have been abandoned. Just think of a small child crying. If we respond by saying, "I am upset," will the child feel any comfort or relief? If we hear a teenager's anger and we comment by saying, "I'm angry," we are unlikely to have an effect other than to make them angrier. Similarly, when an ashamed part says, "I'm worthless," simply echoing those words only reconfirms the part's belief in its lack of worth.

## Repairing Disconnection: How to Listen and Build Attachment Bonds

To develop a trusting relationship, our parts—like all human beings—need someone to respond to them. By replacing "I'm freaked out" with "There's a part of me who's freaking out," we signal to the part that we've heard them, which often brings some immediate relief. This calming effect is stronger when we respond to a parts' complaints with a tone of genuine concern about their feelings: "You're really upset about something—I can tell. What's bothering you?" Our parts need what any distressed human being would need: a caring person who will ask concerned questions, respond in a way that communicates "I get it," or try out different supportive responses until there is a *repair* in that person's state.

Children and adults alike believe the reassuring words of others only if they sense that they are believed, understood, cared about, or important to someone. Empty reassurances not only fail to comfort parts, but they are often a trigger, evoking emotional memories of abusers whose reassurances were a way of grooming the child. We can say the right words, but without empathy and attunement, our words literally fall on deaf ears.

In daily life, adults rarely speak to a two-year-old the same way they would a sixteen-year-old. When we communicate with little children, we use simpler language, express concern not just verbally but with our body language, and choose words familiar to them, such as *scary, bad people, mad, not fair*, and so on. With teenagers, we must be sufficiently connected to our own rebellious or adolescent selves so that our communication does not come across as condescending.

As we take in the fear, shame, confusion, anger, or vulnerability that lives on in the part and emotionally connect to it without blending with it, our feelings toward it usually soften. When we have truly connected with a part, we understand its painful feelings and care about how it feels: "I feel sad for her," "I want to help him," "I feel protective." Parts don't need much because they have gotten so little. As we feel even a little more protective or empathetic, they feel it.

Because communication involves reciprocity—an experience that is missing from the lives of most traumatized individuals—you must concentrate on the back-and-forth communication between you and the parts. Ask, "What's it like for you to feel that I feel bad for you?" Remind yourself that you are giving this part something special. This part isn't used to others caring for it. As you express concern about its feelings, you can feel this part relax, breathe, and even smile. As this mutual connection is built interaction by interaction, this dialogue must continue. Let the part know that it warms your heart to hear that your presence feels good to it, or that it feels special because you are the first person to ever apologize for hurting it.

The greatest obstacle to successfully repairing the distress of our trauma-related parts is our automatic tendency to blend with them and identify with their feelings. Because our emotions and theirs are experienced in the same body and mind, they continue to feel like *our* feelings, not a part's feelings. Even after we understand the concept of parts and can identify them, we continue to blend despite what we know. Unblending from the self-blame and self-doubt held by different parts can be equally, if not more, challenging. It is difficult to question beliefs that have felt familiar and true for many years, even if we can intellectually understand them as coming from a part. To build relationships with our parts, we have to consistently unblend from them and be interested in what they are telling us, rather than agreeing with them. We have to understand that it is easier for human beings to believe they are bad than to believe they are alone in a dangerous world. It is also easier for them to be submissive when they are flooded with shame and self-loathing.

There are two crucial skills you need to develop to embrace the parts whose ingenious use of their defensive responses helped you survive. First, you must learn to observe the signs of being blended with part and practice the skills of unblending (as discussed in chapter 4). Second, you must find a way to access the compassion that you readily extend to others, even strangers, but often struggle to direct toward your own parts. To heal the wounds of trauma, you must be able to feel for these younger parts and overcome your habits of disowning, disparaging, or avoiding them.

In secure, non-traumatic attachment, there are moments of attunement—when both the child and parent settle into a deeply relaxed and calm state. In these moments, the child's small body melts into the parent's grown-up body, and they are both caught up in mutual gazing, smiling, and laughing. These moments feel blissful to both parties. Most of all, they feel safe. In the human brain and body, this sense of safety is neurobiologically linked with our ventral vagal system, also known as the social engagement system (Porges, 2011). This neural system controls the muscles of the face, our eyes and eyelids, the larynx for speech, the middle ear for hearing, and the tilting and turning movements of the head and neck.

Until you can smile at your parts, gaze at them kindly, and speak to them from your heart, they can't feel safe. You may be talking to them, but your social engagement system is still turned off. For children too young to protect themselves and dependent upon those who care for them, attachment equals safety. *For you to feel truly safe now requires that your parts feel safe.*

## From Fear to Feeling: Practicing Compassion for Parts

Avoiding and disowning your parts was an automatic—and necessary—response to an unsafe environment, making it hard to overcome. Try not to believe any feelings of disgust, anger, or judgment toward these parts. These feelings developed to keep your parts at a distance so you could survive emotionally and psychologically. They are instinctive and not a reflection of your deeply felt ethical belief system. If they were, you would reject and judge everyone who has been hurt or is vulnerable.

You may struggle the most when distressed parts require compassion in order to feel safe or soothed. It is challenging to notice distressing feelings as parts, to use the language of parts so they can feel heard, and to be curious and interested in them. Without a doubt, it is hard to learn to unblend from parts and stay with them in that unblended state. But all of that is usually less intimidating than being asked to connect with the parts. Though it may be hard, for the wounded parts to heal, you must allow yourself to empathize with them.

You can start with something easy. Using simple somatic interventions that convey commitment and compassion to your parts generally feels less intimidating than offering empathy for their intense emotions. When your parts are anxious or distressed, notice what happens to their distress if you place a hand over your heart or over the spot where you feel the part's distress. This simple gesture sends a message to the parts: "I hear you—I get it." You don't have to feel empathy. All you have to do is make the movement.

When there are intense inner conflicts between parts or when they are all talking at once, notice what happens if you open your arms and make a big circle as if you're about to catch a giant beach ball. Imagine it as a container for all the parts' feelings, all their points of view, all their beliefs, and all their needs. This gesture opens the chest, sending the message: "All are welcome." The parts can breathe a sigh of relief. They feel a sense of welcome.

Many of us can express an intellectual understanding of our parts. What is much more difficult is making a felt connection that communicates empathic understanding. Here is one small step toward emotionally meeting a part without getting overwhelmed: Imagine taking a distressed part *under your wing*. Putting an arm around someone in distress is very familiar and easy for most of us. That is the "wing" we can offer to the parts. That image conveys connection to young parts but not so much vulnerability that protector parts are threatened by it. It provides a way to support the parts without feeling pressure to care for them. You don't have to like them. You are just offering an open arm and a helping hand. Offering to provide a wing conveys a sense of safety without your risking very much to do it.

Use **Worksheet 14** to practice taking parts "under your wing." Make several copies of this worksheet so you can work on what it's like to offer this repair to more than one part.

When we are blended with parts and lose touch with our adult perspective and capacities, it feels undeniably true that we would never be able to care for our parts, never have the confidence to make decisions, never be able to feel care for any part connected to the traumatic past. But when we offer a wing to a younger part of ourselves, it feels harmless. It's an action that doesn't require effort or faith. Imagine holding your arm open like a wing or simply make that gesture. Notice how easy it is to do. Making the gesture communicates without words. Because it is a somatic communication, it avoids having to think about what it might mean for you to take someone under your wing. There is no commitment on your part to care for them, but the movement speaks directly to the parts' deeply felt need for care and protection.

## Providing Healing Experiences

The goal of this work is to repair the damage left by the past and heal the parts that still carry the traumatic injuries. Traumatic environments involve not only harmful, inappropriate experiences but also the loss of positive experiences that are just as crucial for children to feel safe: trust, safety, comfort, reassurance, protection, joy, and delight.

The provision of a missing experience, of course, does not involve the actual event. There is no way for your five-year-old part to go back to the first day of school and have someone there to hold its hand. But what you can do is to make an emotional, physically felt connection to that five-year-old self now. This part is still alive inside you, and it is still feeling the fears it had then. Imagine that little girl or boy. For a moment, create a felt sense of you being there with this part, taking its hand, and understanding its hesitation or fear. You each have an opportunity to be aware of the other: What is it like for you to feel that little child next to you? What happens for the child when you reach for its hand? How does that little hand feel in your big hand? What's it like for the child to feel your enjoyment in holding that hand?

The key to developing an emotional connection with your parts is to notice them with compassion, which counteracts the traumatic past. The part feels the searing pain of shame but is soothed by your comforting presence. You feel for that ashamed part but are not overwhelmed by its pain or tempted to run from it. You no longer feel the need to alienate your parts in that moment. There are no overwhelming emotions or horrifying images from which distance is needed. And the effect of your presence on the young part can feel warm and good.

## Building Attachment Repair

Parts, like all children, need to feel held in the mind of their caregivers, to feel seen, to have their feelings noticed, validated, and comforted. Our young parts need to be consistently acknowledged by us enough to feel that they matter to someone. They no longer need to feel defensive or heartbroken. We are there now. That is the beginning step.

But attachment isn't about providing our parts with one good moment in a lifetime of trauma; it requires ongoing presence. For the parts to feel secure in our attachment, we need to see them, hear them, and be there on a daily basis. Here are some attachment-building activities you can try:

- Put out a picture of yourself at the age you sense that this younger part may be.
- Go to a store to find something comforting: a stuffed animal for your younger parts, a furry blanket for adult parts.
- Carry a small object (e.g., a stone or tiny toy animal) that symbolizes this part as a way of holding it close.
- Say hello to the parts each morning, checking to see how they are doing *before* they get triggered and force you to notice them.

One of the key experiences missing in the lives of traumatized individuals is having people who delight in them or feel for them when they are upset. In secure attachment, parents find joy in caring for and engaging with their children, despite the stress of childrearing. But when we have experienced a traumatic environment that lacks secure attachment, we may have never had the experience of being valued and loved for who we truly are. As a result, parts have a deep hole in their hearts that can only heal when they feel your sense of interest, delight, and caring. When you communicate to your parts that it gives you pleasure to comfort or support them, that is a reparative moment that contradicts the years of neglect and abuse.

Don't feel pressured to go through the motions in an attempt to "get it right." Attachment is not built on doing things perfectly. It is built moment by moment, piece by piece. While those moments of heart-to-heart connection between your parts and your compassionate self are important, the most important ingredient in lasting change is the repetition of this new way of being with your parts. This is how attachment is formed, whether it is attachment between a baby and parent or attachment between you and your parts.

**Worksheet 15** provides a chance to begin getting to know and understand your younger selves and to welcome them. It also helps you identify parts that are hostile or unaccepting of younger parts and that might block your efforts at connection.

## Rupture and Repair of Internal Attachment Relationships

Knowing that healing cannot result from reexperiencing old emotional pain shifts the direction of trauma therapy. Truly felt self-acceptance and self-compassion can only develop when our young, wounded parts experience the safety of unconditional attachment, when they sense that they now have a protector and advocate. It is our job to keep the ultimate purpose of this work in mind: repairing the feeling memories and traumatic attachment that our parts communicate through their shame, fear, sadness, anger, or emotional pain.

Bruce Ecker, a highly respected expert on traumatic memory, tells us that healing traumatic memory can only occur when we have felt experiences that contradict the past. He argues that we have to experience "living knowledge that is fundamentally incompatible with the [old] model of reality" (Ecker et al., 2012, p. 29), and we have to do so repeatedly with our Noticing Brains online as our witness. It isn't remembering the past that heals. It is *contradicting* the past.

Whatever your relationship to your parts, the building blocks of attachment repair remain the same:

- **Recognize uncomfortable feelings as a part.** As you notice any emotional distress, negative thoughts, or physical reactions to a trigger, say, "There's a part of me that's really overwhelmed by shame right now." Being recognized is a contradicting experience.
- **Unblend from the part if you notice that you're blended.** Simply noticing the part (and noticing yourself observing the part) settles your feelings and often the part's as well. Unblending is a reparative experience because parts become real to you when you unblend from them. It is also a gift: When you become aware of your awareness of the part, it can feel that someone is there.
- **Try to elicit a felt sense of each part,** not an intellectual interpretation. Notice how this part speaks to you through feelings, words, or physical sensations—that's its way of communicating. Let it know that you're listening. Being listened to is an experience your parts are unlikely to have ever had.
- **Care about how the part is feeling.** While blending with a part can feel very painful, simply caring about how that part feels is easier. It's easy to care about the distress of most other people. When you see a child crying in the supermarket or a person looking weary or stressed, you feel for them. Communicating care to them with your attention and interest is a very new contradictory experience for parts.
- **Be curious about the experience you have together.** Notice what it's like for the part to feel you there, to feel your interest and concern. Stay curious. Does it feel good to the part? Weird? Is the part hesitant to trust you? Or is it thrilled that you are there? Notice that it feels good to have an experience together that is not blending!
- **Cultivate trust.** Let the part know you understand how hard it is to trust someone because of how much it's been hurt. Communicate to it that you know—really, really know—why it might be afraid to trust you. You do know why your parts are afraid to trust, why they doubt themselves, why they are angry or sad or judgmental. Even if you have few memories, you probably do know why they feel as they do. When the part senses that you get it, that is a deeply reparative experience. In that past, no one understood or even tried to understand.
- **Use what doesn't work as an attachment-building moment.** Repairs are even more powerful when they arise from relational setbacks. If the part is angry that it's taken so much time for you to show up, acknowledge it. It's been a long wait. When parts back away or shut you out for fear of getting hurt, acknowledge them. Offer them what no one ever did: respect for their

feelings, apologies for mistakes, time to get to know you, and the commitment to stay as long as that part needs you.

- **Avoid the tendency to forget about the parts when things are calm.** With healthy attachment, we nurture our connections in both good times and bad. You would never wait for your children to cry or yell before paying attention to how they are doing. In fact, attuned parents take anticipatory action to prevent their children from getting fussy or overwhelmed. Inside you, there are parts listening to every word you speak, who need to know that they will not be forgotten again as they always have been. As you are reading this, check in with those parts and see how they are doing now. The only way they'll know they won't be forgotten is for you to not forget them. That is another reparative experience that contradicts the past.

As you repeat these steps over and over again, it will become easier for you to feel more spontaneously caring and compassionate toward your parts. They, in turn, will find it easier to trust you, to feel safer in the world, and to feel welcome at long last. That is healing.

## Conclusion

The true repair of trauma begins when we show up, day after day, in relationship with the parts of us who once had no one. While our wounded parts adapted to survive abandonment, fear, and pain, they now look to us to offer a new reality—one where they are heard, seen, and comforted. Healing is not a single act of compassion, but a commitment to presence and protection, repeated in small but powerful moments. As we cultivate these connections with our parts, we are not just undoing the harm of the past; we are building a new inner world—one grounded in trust, kindness, and the kind of love that trauma taught us to fear. Every time we listen, notice, and care, we offer living proof that it's safe now and that no part will ever be left behind again.

Worksheet 14

# Taking a Part Under Your Wing

Notice what happens if you bring your curiosity, calm, compassion, or even courage to a part in distress. What is the result?

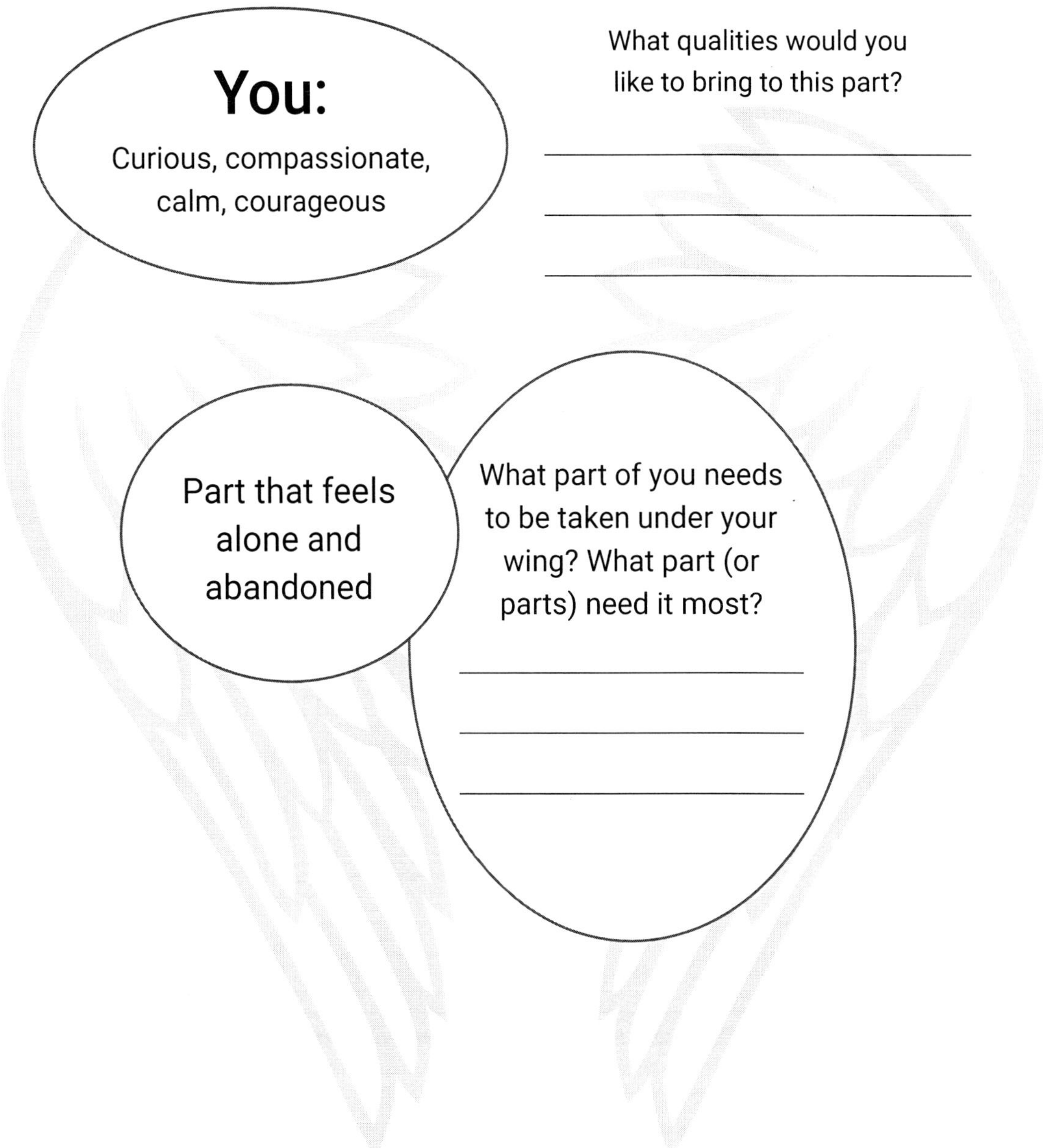


Take a vulnerable part under your wing so they feel less alone and more protected in a dangerous world.

Worksheet 15

# Welcoming Your Younger Selves

Use this worksheet to develop a clearer picture of a child part that is often in distress. The part doesn't have to be connected to any specific event—just to the unsafe environment—and is still struggling.

## Younger Self

How old is this child? What are its feelings and body language telling you? What is this child still worried about?

When you imagine your younger self, how do you feel toward them?

______________________________

______________________________

______________________________

If you notice any judgment or negative reactions, assume that the hostility comes from a different part. What do you notice about that part?

______________________________

______________________________

______________________________

## Youngest Self

How old is this other child? What is this child still worried or distressed about?

What happens if you welcome this younger self as you would any child?

______________________________

______________________________

______________________________

What happens when you welcome all your younger selves? Is it hard to welcome them? Or easy?

______________________________

______________________________

______________________________

Notice how being welcomed affects them.

CHAPTER 9

# Embracing Our Selves

The practice of mindful noticing has created some space between you and your parts, making it much easier to be curious now that they are less overwhelmed and overwhelming. Cause-and-effect relationships are clearer. What others call *overreactions* you have learned to understand as triggered responses of traumatized parts. By consciously developing a relationship with your parts, you naturally begin to develop less aversion to and more fondness for them—or at least have more perspective toward them. If you have struggled with suicidal feelings, self-harm, eating disorders, or substance abuse, you've had to work particularly hard on building a relationship with parts that are more afraid of vulnerability than they are of death. If you have been labeled as *borderline, resistant*, or *playing the victim*, you know now that these labels simply mean that you have parts that are not seen or understood by mental health professionals. If you have struggled with depression or shame, notice how different it is to understand those feelings as parts who bore the burden of humiliation and hopelessness.

By reading this book, you have taken the time to build a foundation by learning each step in the process, hopefully allowing a slow but steady progression. If, in the past, you have taken great leaps forward, only to take two steps back, followed by another attempt to take a big leap, it means that you were going too fast for some of the parts. Your urgency to make progress might have communicated to these parts, "I just want to rush past them" or "I'm in a hurry to get rid of their feelings."

The active ingredients underlying all trauma-related disorders and symptoms are implicit memories held by our fragmented parts, who experience themselves as still in danger of annihilation, abandonment, or both. Trauma recovery must therefore always include these parts, and it must focus on our *relationship* to the traumatic past. Transforming our relationship with overwhelming events requires being on speaking terms with our parts without the fear of being overwhelmed or engulfed by them. While stabilization requires the ability to notice, identify, and differentiate our parts, the healing of traumatic wounds necessitates an additional step: making an emotional connection to the parts and providing reparative experiences that serve as an antidote to the past.

## Reorganizing Our Relationship to the Past

Developing compassionate relationships with parts who are hurt, lonely, consumed by rage, or frightened and ashamed is a challenging job. Because their emotions are so raw and overwhelming, welcoming them requires tolerating their overwhelming or underwhelming emotions and learning how to remain unblended despite strong emotional and physical impulses to blend. In practical terms, this means practicing the ability to stay curious and mindful in the face of these intense internal struggles until we can grow enough compassion to extend empathy to each part. If we feel too much for the parts, we will become flooded with their emotions. If we feel too little for the parts, we will communicate indifference.

If we can stay present and unblended, and appreciate each part's role in surviving the past, we can offer our wounded selves a healing or loving presence that challenges the experiences of the past. *Loving presence* is a state of being: warm, compassionate, curious, unconditionally accepting, and focused on what is right instead of what's wrong. When we cultivate loving presence, time slows down, our bodies relax, and there is a feeling of warmth—a feeling that all is okay. If we try, we can find something to love in all our parts, even those who are stuck, devaluing, self-destructive, demanding, or overwhelming.

## The Role of Memory

Although processing traumatic memory is not the objective of this work, each time you notice a distressing feeling as a part, you are beginning the process of resolving memory. Although the parts usually communicate their fears, doubts, and longings through emotions and sensations, sometimes memories of specific events come up spontaneously. **Treat memory as a doorway, not a destination.** Let it open into a deeper bond with the part of you who had that experience. The past cannot be made safe then, but it *can* end differently now—with the part safely in the arms of someone safe and caring: you.

Your relationship to the unfinished past often spontaneously transforms when you connect to the felt experience of that part and can feel sadness or protectiveness. Tears spring up unexpectedly, your chest or heart opens, you feel the impulse to reach out to the part, and words of compassion arise naturally. There is a feeling of welcome and attunement—the part in that memory can "come home" now. It's safe. When you can offer that reparative experience authentically and compassionately, the story ends with the part safely in the arms of someone safe and caring. Both you and that part share a feeling of warm and loving connection to each other.

Notice how parts respond when they feel even a little bit of your care and protection. Ask them, "Do you feel safer when I hear you? When I understand?" To be noticed and heard is a reparative experience. When you offer loving presence or even inquire about their feelings, it is also a reparative experience. No one in a traumatic environment expresses interest in a person's feelings. No one asks, "What would help you feel safer?" The more often you express care about their feelings, the safer the parts will feel with you, and the more trust they will build.

*Unable to unblend from parts that were afraid of leaving the house or refused to let her leave the perimeter of her property, Annie tried to go back to work by opening a tutoring business in her home. In that way, she could get around the fears because she wouldn't have to leave the house and the children would come to her for their appointments. However, her ability to create lesson plans for her students was constantly undermined by inexplicable deletions of material from her computer, anxious predictions of failure ("You'll be found out"), and a fear so intense she literally shook like a leaf before her first student arrived. But, instead of blending with these parts, she asked, "What are you afraid of?"*

*After listening for a minute, she realized: "They are worried about so many things! They are afraid making a mistake—of not knowing enough—but they are also worried about having someone in the house."*

*Then she remembered what it meant when people came into her childhood home. She asked her parts, "Are you worried they will take you somewhere bad or do something bad to you?"*

Her parts were not just worried about being embarrassed or failing. They were worried about being killed or sexually assaulted. Their preventive efforts to keep her in the house let her know they were afraid they might not make it out alive!

*Annie recounted to her therapist, "I understand why they might not want to risk it. I never thought about what it meant from their point of view. I just tried to push through their objections and get the job done. Now I feel bad for them. I didn't mean to scare them."*

In this unblended state, Annie reflected on how dangerous it truly was in her childhood environment, and she became very emotional. She shuddered as she considered the enormity of a world in which the majority of adults—from family to neighbors to the fathers of her friends—exploited and assaulted young girls. "It's hard to remember how bad it was, and I kept trying not to remember. But that probably freaked out my parts even more. If I didn't remember that it was a dangerous world, how were they going to be protected?"

*Spontaneously, she announced to her parts, "I would never let anyone in this house who would hurt you—*never. *No one bad is ever allowed in this house. If I'm with you, I will never,* ever *allow anyone to harm you." A calm began to settle in her body. The parts could hear the emotion in her voice, and they believed her.*

The sense of safety Annie experienced in her quiet country home life—in a different state and decade—was not shared by her parts. She discovered that her parts still felt the constant threat of abuse. While the distance in time and place mattered to *her* adult mind, it did not yet register in *their* bodies. Naming that mismatch helped her understand why her protectors held the line so fiercely and why present-day reassurance had to be *felt*, not argued.

When Annie remembered the meaning of her parts' alarm reactions and reassured them by staying unblended and present, the parts began to relax a little. They could more easily allow her to do her job without interruption because they felt safer. When she periodically lost touch with the felt sense of wanting to protect them and automatically ignored their fears, she immediately experienced a return to inner conflict and overwhelm. Pushing through her parts' fears may have been necessary when she was young, but now it was a cruel reenactment of the traumatic past.

## "Me Now" Versus "That Part of Me Then"

When *going on with normal life* is associated with pushing through or past your parts' trauma responses, it is easy to feel a sense of being an empty shell—as if you're just going through the motions of life. You may conclude that your ability to function represents a "pseudo-self." Annie illustrates how inaccurate that conclusion can be. Believing that she had created a false self, she failed to see how closely her adult values and priorities reflected her true self. Unconsciously, she had made meaning of the past by creating a healthy, compassionate environment in her adult life where her extended family of choice sought refuge and safety.

*Functioning* and *feeling* each represent a different hemisphere of the brain: The left brain prioritizes order, sequence, organization, and present-moment time, while the right brain is driven by emotions and survival instincts. The left brain is more positive in outlook because it has access to facts, while the right brain, though deeply emotional, is more focused on threat (Hanson, 2014). Both hemispheres and priorities are necessary to living a full, rich life.

## Rupture and Repair

Child development researchers have demonstrated that even as infants, our ability to tolerate discomfort and our resilience both increase when we experience *just enough* distress and then are soothed and re-regulated (Tronick, 2007). In the attachment literature, this phenomenon is labeled *rupture and repair.* The child's experience of discomfort is followed by some kind of repair (encouragement, soothing, reassurance, distraction) that reinstates positive feeling states. When this is a repeated experience, the child's resilience increases. They can tolerate more because their little bodies have developed an expectation that repair will come, that someone will soothe the rupture, that good experiences will follow bad, and that fear will be reassured by safety.

For traumatized parts of all ages, however, it is very different. These parts have come to expect that bad experiences are more likely than good, that no one will soothe or protect them, and that their world is not safe. Anything that feels good or safe is likely to be followed by something bad.

A very important principle of internal healing work is that all parts-related difficulties are opportunities to foster a repair of the past. As parts intrude into your awareness with their thoughts, images, and intense emotions, you can pause what you are doing to notice and acknowledge them. Switch from your Thinking Brain to your Noticing Brain. What happens when you recognize these feelings as parts communicating to you instead of thinking about how much you don't want to feel that way? Notice if you are blending with the emotions. If you aren't sure, assume that you are. Take a minute to put up your hands, using one hand to represent the part in distress and the other hand to represent you noticing that part. Using both hands, stay with the part, just noticing it and noticing you. Care about how the part feels without taking on that emotion. Remember that unblending is a gift to the part: When you can notice yourself noticing the part, it can feel that someone is there.

## Communicating Compassion Toward Wounded Parts

Once you are unblended, present, and able to communicate some genuine care for how your parts feel, you are already providing them with a "missing experience" that repairs a piece of the past (Kurtz, 1990). Listening to them, validating their fears, and unblending so that you are in relationship with them are also missing experiences. A missing experience represents what you should have been offered in a safe world with safe attachment figures, whether it is understanding, comfort, protection, or loving presence. Each part will probably need a different missing experience. Each will have different repair needs based on its age, developmental stage, trauma experiences, and specific survival defenses. For example, a fight part might need a sense of control and respect; an attach part might yearn to feel protected, loved, and safe from abandonment; a freeze or fear part might crave safety from harm; a submit part might need to feel worth and purpose; and a flight part might wish for freedom from entrapment.

> Turn to **Worksheet 16** to practice sensing the missing experiences needed by different wounded parts. This is a chance to use your Noticing Brain rather than your Thinking Brain.

Because communication involves reciprocity (another experience missing from the lives of most traumatized individuals), an important part of this process involves noticing how the parts respond to what you offer. For example: "What's it like for the little boy to feel your sadness for him? He isn't used to people feeling for him" or "What's it like for the little girl to hear that you want to protect her? Does that feel good or a little scary?" Most often, the part will express positive feelings, either in words or in emotions and body sensations. You can ask, "What's it like for the part to hear someone expressing concern about its feelings?" Often, you can feel a spontaneous response: relaxation, warmth, a smile, a deep breath. It's important to verbally acknowledge these responses so the parts can hear you: "It feels good to him to feel that someone cares about his feelings, huh?" or "Yes, she can breathe—knowing I want to protect her must be a relief."

Equally important is the question that should always follow: "And what's it like for you to feel how much it means to him?" If you are touched by the part's reaction to what you offer, let it know that. Ask it what it's like to hear you say it warms your heart to have this connection with it. Remember that one important missing experience for traumatized individuals is being delighted in or felt for. When parts feel your empathetic "getting it" as an emotional communication, there is relief and even joy. Despite the misgivings of protector parts and the fear of trust in young parts, traumatized parts are longing for these reparative experiences that fill holes in their hearts.

When the part has shown you an image or there is some connection to memory, validate what it has communicated: "Now, I get how afraid you are of leaving the house and being seen, and I understand it completely. It wasn't a good idea then to have people watching you—it was creepy" or "I completely understand—it wasn't a good idea to try something new unless you were absolutely sure you knew what would happen." You don't have to validate the event, but the parts do need you to validate their experience as a result of those events.

Stay connected to the reparative experience you are providing to this traumatized part, whether it is the felt sense of being understood, the experience of being genuinely moved by their hurt and fear, or the somatic experience of warmth, muscles relaxing, and heart rate slowing. As trust builds between you and this part, protector parts may intrude and try to distract from these moments of attunement. When protectors feel threatened by your warmth, loving presence, softness, and vulnerability, the critical voices of fight parts often intervene, alongside annoyed parts, confused parts, or anxious parts. These protectors believe that relaxing their guard is dangerous, and they are afraid of increasing vulnerability. These are pivotal moments because they provide a chance to offer the protectors a missing experience. Remember that healing is not just about your relationships to vulnerable parts. It requires creating a healing environment for *all* the parts.

It makes sense that fight and flight parts might be suspicious, mistrustful, cynical, or sabotaging. It is understandable that some protector parts—particularly those whose abusers were exceptionally sadistic, manipulative, or malevolent—would be more vigilant in armoring themselves against taking in anything positive or allowing vulnerable parts to let down their guard.

## Working with Protectors: Power, Respect, and Role

Therefore, you want to notice any interruption in attunement as the actions of a protector. Name it and validate it: "Of course the protector would be worried about all these positive feelings. It doesn't want me to let down my guard." You want to acknowledge the protector's role, thank it for its efforts over the years, and invite it to continue standing guard. These parts were often scapegoated for speaking truth to power or for refusing to submit. In a world controlled by abusers, the only actual "power" they had was to distrust and harden themselves—and to try to harden the other parts. When you express appreciation for them and understand and honor their contributions to your survival, you cultivate a sense of attunement with them without making them feel uncomfortably vulnerable.

Protector parts need attachment too. Like wary teenagers, they reject comfort and reassurance and don't want to be treated as vulnerable. But they still need respect, gratitude, and persistent contact that proves you won't give up on them. Giving protectors conscious, prosocial *missions*—setting boundaries, scheduling rest, and screening relationships—balances vulnerability with strength, allowing them to feel respected for their role while also encouraging them to soften their defenses over time.

Sometimes, even when traumatized parts feel nourished, warmed, or held by our care, they suddenly pause and pull back, afraid to believe that it is true (or unwilling to let themselves believe it to be true). How can they trust someone who says they care when all they have ever known is a lack of caring?

Your job is to normalize and validate any part's fears of trusting you: "This is so new—no wonder it's hard to trust. Does it feel good to know that I feel for you? Or is it a little uncomfortable?" Sometimes, you will feel the part wanting to trust you, wanting to believe you. You might notice that it keeps relaxing into you and then stiffening and pulling back. Always assume that any traumatized part wants to trust you, and always remember that the trauma necessitated it learning to mistrust. Ask the part, "Would you like to trust me? Would you like to believe that I won't leave, that I won't hurt you?" This is an opportunity to provide a contradictory experience for the part: It was never safe to express its negative or positive feelings. Being able to communicate its fears and doubts, along with its wish to be loved—and having both be accepted and understood—is an important part of the healing process.

The importance of using embodied communication with your parts cannot be stressed too much:

- "Let the little boy know with your feelings and your body that you completely understand why he feels that way."
- "Use your feelings to tell her that you're here now and that you mean to stay."
- "Just hold him gently so he gets the message that he's not alone."

Your physical and emotional presence communicate reassurance and safety in a way that words alone cannot convey.

## Creating a New Purpose and Mission for Each Part

When we consciously and voluntarily give protector parts more power and control, there are many positive benefits. It creates a better balance of vulnerability versus strength, and protector parts are more willing to allow access to young, wounded, or innocent parts. In addition, internal communication improves, and we become more resourced, self-protective, and better boundaried—all from an unlikely source: our own fight and flight parts. Every part contributes resources that are important in any adult's life, whether it's the ability to be vulnerable or the ability to stand our ground.

> Turn to **Worksheet 17, *Appreciating the Gifts of Each Part***. As parts are healed by your care, and their reactions are no longer extreme, you can begin to appreciate the positive contributions of each part. Feeling recognized for their strengths and value is another healing experience for your parts.

Researchers have noted that one key trait of mothers who promote secure attachment in their children is their ability to resonate with the baby's state, modulate their own emotions to prevent the infant's distress or enhance positive mood, and mirror both states back to the baby (Kim et al., 2014). This mirroring, paired with the mother's corresponding feelings of concern, enjoyment, empathy, or warmth, communicates two messages: "I understand" and "I can help."

However, if the mother simply mirrors the infant's emotional state without offering support, both may become stuck in the same distress. These are the moments when mothers become blended with their babies. If the mother only reflects back a more positive state of her own, the baby has no comforting sense of being understood. The mother's mirroring will seem more like an empty reassurance: "I don't understand what you're feeling, but don't worry—you'll feel better soon."

You can apply the concept of attunement, which was discussed in previous chapters, to the relationship between you and your parts. When you blend with the feelings of a wounded part, it leaves that part alone with the distressing emotions, much like offering disembodied words of reassurance or hope. Not only is it crucial for parts to feel a visceral sense that you get how scared, ashamed, angry, or hurt they are—they also need to feel the emotional effect of your curiosity, compassion, calm, strength, and protectiveness.

Each time you attune to the wounded part's unmet need, fear, or painful emotion and offer a missing experience, attachment bonds are built, piece by piece, experience by experience. For infants, it is the act of the baby calming and relaxing into the parent's arms that generates the shared felt sense of closeness, safety, and warmth that we label *attunement*.

When this compassionate and caring "you" and your wounded part share repeated experiences of feeling safe and welcome, both of you will experience the deep sensory and emotional connection evoked by your mutual attunement. Although it is now many years later, this part can feel securely held at last. You are offering this part a bodily and emotional state that conveys love and safety, the certainty of feeling cherished, and the comfort of the warm felt presence of another. At the worst of times, you can be there for yourself—like a parent to whom someone can turn at any age or stage of life.

*Earned secure attachment* is a concept that has been discussed for many years in the literature (Roisman et al., 2001) that refers to our unique ability as humans to heal our own wounds by evoking the healing experiences that have been missing from our lives. Regardless of how traumatic our early attachment experiences may have been, there is an opportunity for us as adults to *earn* the secure attachment that was not available to us when we were young and dependent on the attachment status of our parents for a sense of security. Now, we can offer that security to our parts. When they feel it, we can feel it.

## Conclusion

You have done the hardest part: You stayed. You listened when it was painful. You showed up for parts that expected to be forgotten again. This work is not about becoming someone else—it is about becoming the trustworthy, caring presence you always needed. Each act of noticing, each moment of kindness, each invitation to connect rewrites the old story. Now, you are the one who gets to say, "I'm here, and I won't leave." That is how healing happens. That is what it means to embrace all of your selves.

Worksheet 16

# Offering Healing Experiences to Parts

To offer your parts an experience that helps them heal requires your Noticing Brain and your compassion. Make sure that you can feel the wish to offer them some relief or care . . .

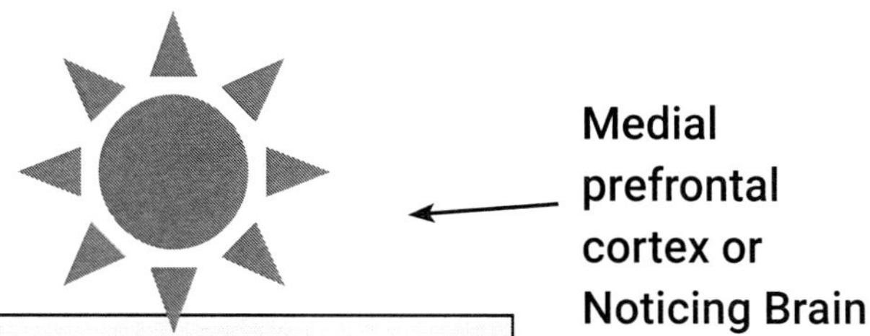


**You**

| Fight Part | Flight Part | Freeze Part | Submit Part | Cry-for-Help Part |
|---|---|---|---|---|
| What is the missing experience for the fight part? | What is the missing experience for the flight part? | What is the missing experience for the freeze part? | What is the missing experience for the ashamed, hopeless part? | What is the missing experience for the cry-for-help part that wants closeness? |
| ______ | ______ | ______ | ______ | ______ |
| ______ | ______ | ______ | ______ | ______ |
| ______ | ______ | ______ | ______ | ______ |
| ______ | ______ | ______ | ______ | ______ |
| ______ | ______ | ______ | ______ | ______ |
| ______ | ______ | ______ | ______ | ______ |

Notice how it feels inside you when you offer a part the experience it has been waiting for.

Worksheet 17

# Appreciating the Gifts of Each Part

As your parts feel safer and their wounds heal, you can begin to appreciate the gifts each part offers, the qualities unique to that part that enrich your life and offer the part a new role in it.

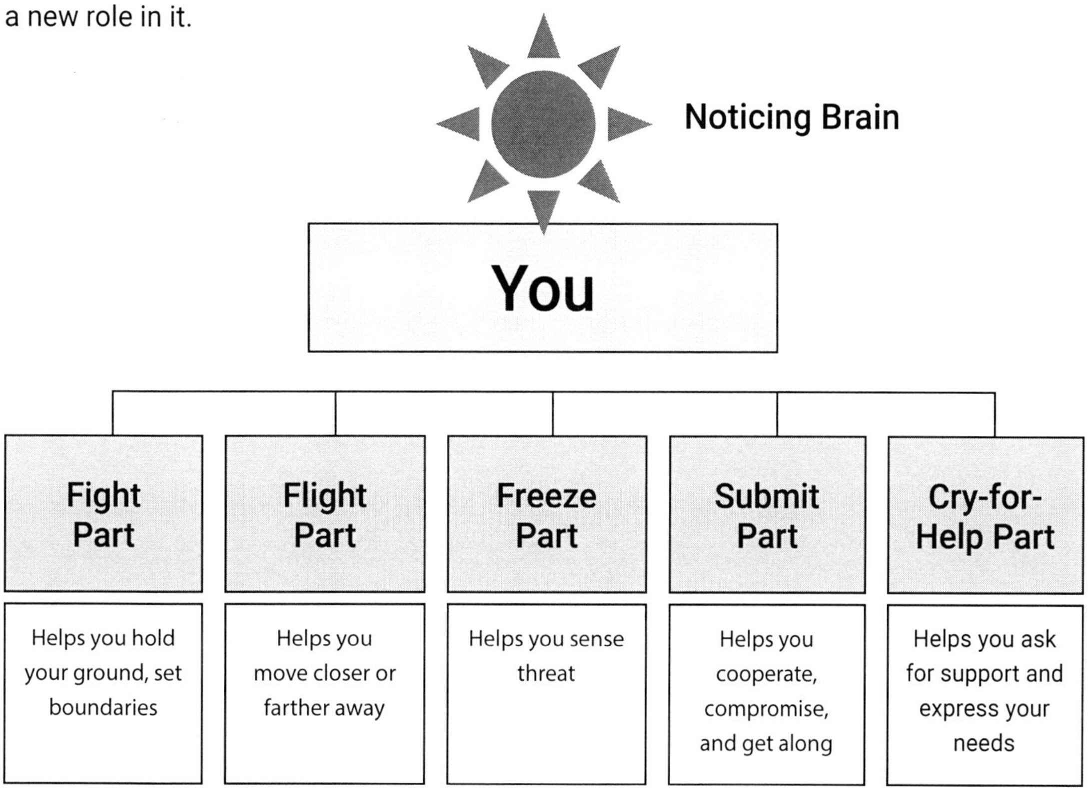


How is each part's gift helping you become the person you were meant to be?

____________________________________________________________

____________________________________________________________

____________________________________________________________

____________________________________________________________

____________________________________________________________

____________________________________________________________

____________________________________________________________

# References

For your convenience, purchasers can download and print selected resources from this book at **pesipubs.com/fragmented**

Damasio, A. (1999). *The feeling of what happens: Body and emotion in the making of consciousness.* Harcourt.

Damis, L. F. (2022). The role of implicit memory in the development and recovery from trauma-related disorders. *NeuroSci, 3*(1), 63–88. https://doi.org/10.3390/neurosci3010005

Ecker, B., Ticic, R., & Hulley, L. (2012). *Unlocking the emotional brain: Eliminating symptoms at their roots using memory reconsolidation.* Routledge.

Fisher, J. (2021). *Transforming the living legacy of trauma: A workbook for survivors and therapists.* PESI Publishing.

Hanson, R. (2014). *Hardwiring happiness: The new brain science of contentment, calm, and confidence.* Harmony Publications.

Kim, S., Fonagy, P., Allen, J., Martinez, S., Iyengar, U., & Strathearn, L. (2014). Mothers who are securely attached in pregnancy show more attuned infant mirroring 7 months postpartum. *Infant Behavior and Development, 37*(4), 491–504. https://doi.org/10.1002/da.20751

Kurtz, R. (1990). *Body-centered psychotherapy: The Hakomi method* (Updated ed.). Life Rhythm.

Liotti, G. (2011). Attachment disorganization and the controlling strategies: An illustration of the contributions of attachment theory to developmental psychopathology and to psychotherapy integration. *Journal of Psychotherapy Integration, 21*(3), 232–252. https://doi.org/10.1037/a0025422

Ogden, P. (2021). *The pocket guide to sensorimotor psychotherapy in context.* W. W. Norton.

Ogden, P., & Fisher, J. (2015). *Sensorimotor psychotherapy: Interventions for trauma and attachment.* W. W. Norton.

Perl, O., Duek, O., Kulkarni, K. R., Gordon, C., Krystal, J. H., Levy, I., Harpaz-Rotem, I., & Schiller, D. (2023). Neural patterns differentiate traumatic from sad autobiographical memories in PTSD. *Nature Neuroscience, 26*, 2226–2236. https://doi.org/10.1038/s41593-023-01483-5

Phillips, M., & Frederick, C. (1995). *Healing the divided self: Clinical and Ericksonian hypnotherapy for post-traumatic and dissociative conditions.* W.W. Norton.

Porges, S. W. (2011). *The polyvagal theory: Neurophysiological foundations of emotions, attachment, communication, and self-regulation.* W. W. Norton.

Roisman, G. I., Padron, E., Sroufe, L. A., & Egeland, B. (2002). Earned-secure attachment status in retrospect and prospect. *Child Development, 73*(4), 1204–1219. https://doi.org/10.1111/1467-8624.00467

Schwartz, R. C., & Sweezy, M. (2020). *Internal family systems therapy* (2nd ed.). Guilford Press.

Tronick, E. (2007). *The neurobehavioral and social-emotional development of infants and children.* W. W. Norton.

van der Hart, O., Nijenhuis, E. R. S., & Steele, K. (2006). *The haunted self: Structural dissociation and the treatment of chronic traumatization.* W. W. Norton.

van der Kolk, B. A. (2014). *The body keeps the score: Brain, mind and body in the healing of trauma.* Viking Press.

van der Kolk, B. A., Hopper, J., & Osterman, J. (2001). Exploring the nature of traumatic memory: Combining clinical knowledge with laboratory methods. *Journal of Aggression, Maltreatment & Trauma, 4*(2), 9–31. https://doi.org/10.1300/J146v04n02_02

# About the Author

**Janina Fisher, PhD,** is a licensed clinical psychologist and former instructor at Harvard Medical School. An international expert on the treatment of trauma, she is an executive board member of the Trauma Research Foundation and a patron of the John Bowlby Centre. Dr. Fisher is the author of *Healing the Fragmented Selves of Trauma Survivors*, *Transforming the Living Legacy of Trauma*, and *The Living Legacy of Trauma Flip Chart*, as well as numerous peer-reviewed journal articles, and is coauthor with Pat Ogden of *Sensorimotor Psychotherapy*. She is best known for her work on integrating mindfulness-based and somatic interventions into trauma treatment. Her treatment model, Trauma-Informed Stabilization Treatment (TIST), is now being taught around the world. More information can be found on her website: www.janinafisher.com.